D1565601

Lean Innovation

Claus Sehested · Henrik Sonnenberg

Lean Innovation

A Fast Path from Knowledge to Value

 Springer

Claus Sehested
Implement Consulting Group P/S
Slotsmarken 16
2970 Hørsholm
Denmark
cs@implement.eu

Henrik Sonnenberg
Implement Consulting Group P/S
Slotsmarken 16
2970 Hørsholm
Denmark
hso@implement.eu

ISBN 978-3-642-15894-0   e-ISBN 978-3-642-15895-7
DOI 10.1007/978-3-642-15895-7
Springer Heidelberg Dordrecht London New York

Library of Congress Control Number: 2010936266

Cover design: WMXDesign GmbH, Heidelberg

Cover graphics: IMPERIET/Lonnie Hamburg, Copenhagen

Printed on acid-free paper

Springer is part of Springer Science+Business Media (www.springer.com)

Preface

In 15th-century Spain, the Port of Cádiz was a hub of ship builders, sailmakers, sailors, merchants, captains and rich noblemen. All these men had one thing in common – they shared the dream of unknown territory where great riches awaited. And fueled by this dream, they embarked on great adventures. They did not always chart the right course, were hit by storms and suffered disasters along the way. They learned new things and had to improvise with whatever they had at hand. And yet, because the captain and his crew believed in their dream and because they worked together to achieve a common goal, the seafarers ultimately did return to Spain with great riches.

Lean innovation is about discovering new territory and about efficient realization of a dream. We enjoy working in environments where focused action transforms dreams into results. Strategy and innovation have been our professional passion for more than ten years. And during that time, we have designed development organizations and innovation processes, produced product strategies and developed products. We have coached leaders, project managers and specialists in innovation work, and we have participated in development projects as sparring partners and coaches. All of this has taught us that innovation has the strongest impact on the bottom line, and creates the highest employee satisfaction when the company does a good job in a few key areas:

- Innovation work should be based on a good understanding of the customer's situation and needs.
- Participants and departments need to show respect, openness and responsibility.
- Management should ignite an innovation dream that is strong enough to overcome the challenges that arise during the process.
- Management should have an active and visible management style that helps the innovation projects achieve their goals.
- Progress, results and structure should be kept in focus so that good ideas and good intentions are not lost along the way.

In our experience, the companies that manage to be both 'soft' and 'hard' at the same time achieve the best innovation results.

We want to show you how leaders can work with these two aspects and reduce the distance between themselves and their knowledge workers while keeping their eye on the target.

This book is based on the premise that it is possible to improve knowledge and development work. No matter how good you are, you can always be better. Lean innovation is about creating an innovation system that continuously improves itself, so it becomes the company's primary competitive weapon.

Our work as management consultants has given us the opportunity to observe innovation processes in many different sectors, companies and functions. We want to express our thanks to the companies that have asked our advice on tackling innovation challenges. Our experiences from working with them form the foundation for this book.

We would especially like to thank the companies that have contributed directly to this book: ECCO, LINAK, Ramboll Oil & Gas, Exhausto and Coloplast have helped bring this book alive. Thanks to Aage Andersen, Johannes M. Knudsen and Jens Christian Meier from ECCO, Claus Hegelund Sørensen and Tom Toft Krag from LINAK, Anders Rødgaard Knudsen from Ramboll Oil & Gas, Karsten Lund from Exhausto and John Raabo Nielsen and Niels Fogelstrøm from Coloplast.

At Implement Consulting Group, we work in a unique professional environment that has allowed us to develop the ideas for this book. We would like to thank the many colleagues we have worked with on innovation issues. And special thanks to John Ryding Olsson and Henrik Tufvesson for their critical and constructive feedback on the chapters in this book. We would also like to express our gratitude to Tine Søderberg and Caroline M. Gullacksen for their work on the illustrations and page set-up.

Copenhagen, September 2010
Claus Sehested and Henrik Sonnenberg

Contents

Chapter 7
Projects Create Customer Value 129

Chapter 8
The Role of Project Support in Innovation 159

Part I
Understanding the Background

Introduction

What is Lean Innovation?

'Lean' means thin and well-trimmed. Working with lean means working systematically to eliminate all non-value-adding processes in order to achieve your goals with the least possible effort. Unnecessary work, or waste, is used in this connection as an umbrella term for anything that does not create customer value. In the search for waste, you need to look for anything that 'can't be invoiced'. Waste is what the customer won't pay for. Eliminating waste is also a good idea from the point of view of the employee: No one likes to produce something that isn't used.

Innovation is about creating value by solving problems. Creativity is a prerequisite for problem-solving and is brought into play at various points during the process. But creativity alone is not enough. It needs to be put into a framework ensure that the solutions are actually put to use. Innovation is also about knowledge. At the beginning of an innovation process, the knowledge you have about the problem you are trying to solve is usually limited. Through the process, you learn more about the problem and its possible solutions. And based on this knowledge you choose between different possible solutions. This makes innovation a learning and prioritization process.

In this book, we use the term innovation broadly to include research, R&D, product and service development and other types of development work in both the private and public sectors.

Lean innovation is about working efficiently with knowledge. Put simply, lean innovation is about getting smart fast. Cut to the bone, lean innovation helps a company do three fundamental things. First to 'do the right thing', then to 'do it right' and finally to 'do it better' all the time.

C. Sehested, H. Sonnenberg, *Lean Innovation,* DOI 10.1007/978-3-642-15895-7_1,
© Springer-Verlag Berlin Heidelberg 2011

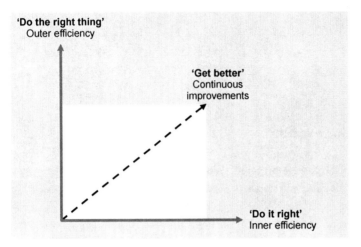

Figure 0.1. Three Paths to Efficiency

'Do the right thing'
Doing the right thing is the easiest way to avoid waste. In innovation, this means using your technical competencies to meet the customer's needs and avoiding over or underdeveloping the solution. In practice, it is about properly communicating expectations to the recipients of the work. This includes both internal and external customers. Because needs and expectations are not static, and because innovation is a learning process, it can be useful to maintain a close dialog with the customers throughout the innovation process.

'Do it right'
Doing it right means optimum planning of the work process that leads to the solution. The challenge in innovation is that the problems you need to solve are always new and therefore require individualized processes, also called value streams. Consequently, it is necessary to create a new value stream every time you create a solution. In innovation, the value stream is the same as the project plan.

'Get better'
Working with lean means continually evaluating your work and making improvements. In fact, it means making continuous improvements an integral part of the way you think. Of course, it is always best to make improvements that have a significant impact, but the need for major improvements can be a symptom that not enough small improvements have been made. When you work

with lean innovation, you create a system and rituals for continuous improvements that become part of your daily routines.

Fast from Knowledge to Value

Why should companies work with lean innovation? Because outside factors make action necessary. In today's globalized world, a company's strategic situation changes very quickly: Market opportunities arise, competition increases and new collaborative networks and customer groups develop. In order to stay ahead of the game, companies need to develop a strategic agility that enables them to capture movements and opportunities in their surroundings and quickly change their strategic course. But this ability is worthless if companies are not also able to react quickly within their organizations. It is crucial that the strategies are transformed into action more quickly.

This places pressure on the innovation process, as it is through this process that a large share of the strategies are realized. Developing faster innovation processes with more predictable output is a strategic necessity. This is where lean plays a central role.

In autumn 1996, James P. Womack and Daniel T. Jones finished their book *Lean Thinking*. It became the starting point of a rather remarkable revolution in production, and people quickly developed a massive interest in the results that could be achieved with lean. And these results were actually being created in an environment that, even before lean, had always focused on improvements, efficiency, measurement and follow-up.

In innovation, the improvement potential is even greater than in production. In a production process, there is a limit to how much costs can be reduced. In an innovation process, however, the primary objective is not to reduce costs. This is not unimportant, of course, but innovation is first and foremost about getting solutions out to the customers quickly and creating solutions that are so innovative that you expand your market or create an entirely new market.

If you consider Figure 0.2 on the improvement potential that exists from identifying a customer need until a solution is delivered, there are more opportunities to bring new thoughts into play early rather than later in the process. The closer you get to the 'delivered solution', the more you are bound by the decisions that have already been made.

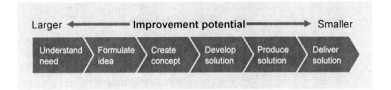

Figure 0.2. Process from Need to Delivered Solution

While lean production deals with creating value in the late phases of the above process, lean innovation is about creating value in the early phases.

Having Your Cake and Eating it Too

Many companies that try to create more value and efficiency in their innovation work discover that the concept of efficiency is rather taboo. Some developers and specialists feel the need for more efficiency is an indirect criticism of their work. And they have no problems explaining to managers, who may be very far removed from the development work, that increasing efficiency would destroy innovation quality. Many well-meaning, but top-down implemented, stream-lining initiatives have failed because the people who were responsible for the changes did not understand the essence of the innovation work.

However, there is a way to overcome these challenges. It requires embracing the paradox between efficiency and creativity and taking a structured approach to solving it. Innovation people are experts at solving paradoxes, because that is the key to all innovative solutions.

It is a common assumption that there is always a trade-off between input and output. To achieve more output, you need a corresponding increase in input. For example, it used to be commonly assumed that a light bulb had to consume more energy in order to produce a stronger light, and that lowering the fat content in food reduces the flavor. The best developers question such conventions and what 'everyone says'. That is what makes working on development projects exciting, and that is the driving force of innovation.

Many talented developers, fueled by big dreams, have rejected existing conventions to create innovative solutions. The developers have moved from 'trade-off' to what we call 'trade-on'. They have solved the paradox. The best innovations make it possible to have your cake and eat it too.

But is it possible to be efficient and creative at the same time? Is it possible to solve the paradox between lean and innovation? Yes, it is. And if you succeed, the potential is practically endless.

Our Aim with this Book

We decided to write a book for managers — both those with daily responsibility for innovation and business development and those who want to stay in touch with developments in the area. With this book, we want to make managers think about their current organizations and reflect on how their own management thinking and behavior influences the organization and the organization's ability to innovate.

This book it not a methodology book, and it does not introduce a complete development system or an exhaustive list of lean methods. The methods described here are only provided to illustrate the points in the book. This book also contains a number of examples of what other companies have done to improve their innovation work.

The Case Companies

The examples of challenges and practical implementation included in this book come from a number of companies that have worked with lean innovation. Before we proceed, we would like to introduce the five case companies:

ECCO aims to be the most recognized brand within innovative and comfortable footwear. The company was founded in 1963 and has revenue of EUR 720 million and 16,000 employees. Today, the company has its own global concept stores, production facilities and development functions.

ECCO's products are based on a unique manufacturing technology in which the sole and the upper are molded together using a special injection technique. The product development takes place in Portugal, Thailand, Denmark and the Netherlands, and involves leading external designers.

LINAK has a vision to improve people's quality of life and working environment through products featuring linear actuators. Actuators are used in such products as automatic height-adjustable desks and hospital beds. LINAK started manufacturing actuators in 1980 and has facilities in China and Denmark. The company has experienced significant growth and has revenue of approx. EUR 270 million and 1,600 employees.

The key to LINAK's success is their ability to find simple and lasting solutions to complex problems in close collaboration with their customers.

Ramboll Oil & Gas is an engineering consultancy firm with the ambition to become one of the world's largest in the sector. Its customers are international energy companies. The firm has revenue of approx. EUR 75 million and 650 employees located in Denmark, Norway, the UAE, India and the UK. It is part of the Ramboll Group, which has a total staff of 8,000 employees.

For Ramboll Oil & Gas, customer-oriented processes represent a strategic competency that is intended to drive growth. The projects require multi-discipline teams working together locally and across offices all over the world.

Exhausto produces ventilation solutions that improve people's health and well-being. The company develops components for ventilation systems. It was established in 1957 and has since grown to 300 employees, with revenue of EUR 54 million. Exhausto has decided that the company should be characterized by the lean concept of 'flow', and that the business processes should be developed through continuous improvements.

Coloplast's goal is to make life easier for people with intimate and personal treatment needs in the areas of ostomy, incontinence and urology. Coloplast, which is headquartered north of Copenhagen, Denmark, has developed and manufactured health care products since 1957. Its annual revenue is now EUR 1.2 billion. The company operates globally and has approx. 7,000 employees.

Coloplast has a unique ability to understand the situations and daily lives of patients and nurses, and to incorporate this knowledge in their innovation work.

In addition to these case companies, the book also contains examples from leading global innovators.

Structure of the Book

The first part of the book discusses what companies can get out of streamlining the innovation process and establishing a basic understanding of both innovation and lean innovation. We then describe lean innovation within the relevant action areas, illustrated with specific examples. Finally, the book examines the challenges companies face when they begin implementing lean innovation.

Chapter 1 explores the potential of streamlining innovation. It presents the case companies' motivation for working with lean innovation along with the results they have achieved.

Chapter 2 takes a closer look at innovation and at what takes place during the innovation processes. It is important to understand the mechanisms in innovation in order to be able to develop the process.

Chapter 3 introduces lean innovation. This chapter presents the key concepts, principles and methods, and they are explained in relation to the mechanisms in innovation.

Chapter 4 presents a model that divides lean innovation into action areas. These are each treated differently, but together they represent a lean innovation system.

Chapter 5 highlights management as an important element in lean innovation. Lean innovation is a management philosophy that impacts how leaders improve their roles and how they choose to behave.

Chapter 6 focuses on portfolio management as an independent action area. It is an overlooked discipline in many companies. However, when handled properly, it can establish a healthy framework for the projects.

Chapter 7 provides a number of tools for ensuring the right focus and cooperation within the projects through commitment from all participants.

Chapter 8 looks to the relationship between the project managers and the support functions that deliver sub-solutions for the projects. How do you ensure good interaction and achieve efficiency in the project activities of the support functions?

Chapter 9 looks forward at the implementation of lean innovation in the company. How do you find the motivation to realize the transformation, and how do you initiate the process?

Chapter 1
The Potential of Lean Innovation

Innovation processes play a key role in realizing a company's strategic ambitions. The strategic need for agility and value creation forces companies to develop their innovation processes. For companies in global competition, the innovation machine needs to be well-oiled in order to produce good results quickly and with great predictability. So, is this the case?

In 2008, Boston Consulting Group (BCG) and *BusinessWeek* asked 3,000 global senior executives whether they were satisfied with the benefit their company obtained from its innovation processes. More than half responded no. Furthermore, more than 60 percent stated that innovative ability was one of the three most important strategic challenges. Innovation is considered important, but is not functioning satisfactorily. So there is room for improvement in a lot of companies.

A closer look at the responses from the senior executives reveals that they consider lengthy development times, a risk-averse culture, difficulties prioritizing ideas and poor coordination within the company to be the biggest obstacles to creating value from innovation. All of these challenges relate to how we lead and organize the innovation processes within the company. It is also interesting that 'lack of good ideas' is far down the list. So the problem is not so much 'what' but rather 'how'. The senior executives see a need to improve the ability to prioritize and execute projects.

C. Sehested, H. Sonnenberg, *Lean Innovation*, DOI 10.1007/978-3-642-15895-7_2,
© Springer-Verlag Berlin Heidelberg 2011

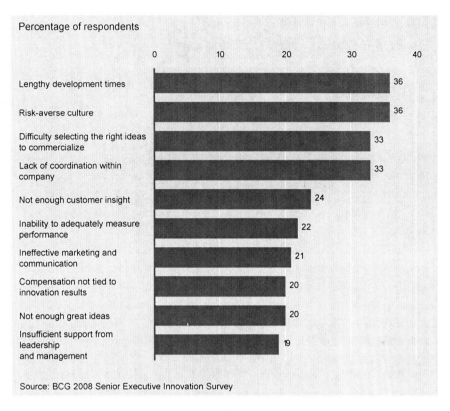

Figure 1.1. The Biggest Obstacles to Creating Value from Investments in Innovation, According to Global Senior Executives

Generating Return on Innovation

As illustrated previously, the potential for value creation is greater for innovation than for production. There is a limit to how much you can achieve by streamlining production. In innovation, there is no upper limit to value creation: "Only the sky is the limit." When it comes to innovation, it is therefore much more interesting to focus on what you get from your investments than on how you can reduce costs. 'Innovation costs' is actually not a very appropriate term because it suggests that innovation is an operational cost that needs to be kept down. 'Innovation investments' is a better term.

And a look at corporate budgets reveals that spending in innovation is far from small change. In 2007, Nokia, in Finland, spent an astronomical EUR 5.3 billion on R&D, corresponding to more than 10 percent of their revenue. Nokia holds 40 percent of the global market for cell phones, and launches approx.

60 new models every year globally – that's more than one cell phone a week. Samsung, HTC and iPhone are constantly challenging Nokia's dominance. So is the fast-growing market for services like music, e-mail, games and apps. In the service area, the complexity and demand for fast execution are even greater than within cell phone hardware. This makes innovation – especially fast innovation – is a strategic key parameter for Nokia.

Looking west from Finland to Sweden, we find Ericsson and Volvo, which also invest impressive sums in innovation. And farther south, we find Denmark and the insulin producer Novo Nordisk. Even though Novo Nordisk is not that big a company on a global scale, it still invests EUR 1 billion on innovation annually and employs 4,600 people in R&D. These four companies are the biggest R&D spenders in Northern Europe. There are more than 20 companies throughout the region that invest more than EUR 100 million a year, each, on developing new products and services.

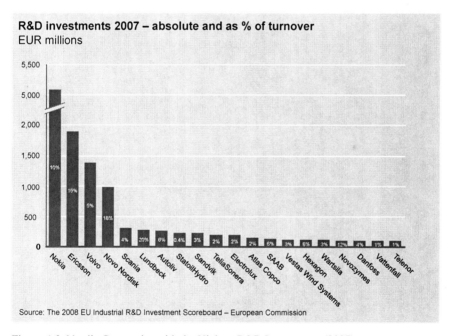

R&D investments 2007 – absolute and as % of turnover
EUR millions

Source: The 2008 EU Industrial R&D Investment Scoreboard – European Commission

Figure 1.2. Nordic Companies with the Highest R&D Investments (2007)

With such significant investments, it seems reasonable to ask whether we are getting enough for our money. Are we making the most efficient use of the funds? Are we innovative in the way we innovate or are we just doing what we usually do? In any case, there is good basis for an ongoing discussion of innovation and efficiency.

The size of a company's R&D investments does not necessarily determine its innovative ability or business success. In 2007, Apple was that of the 50 largest high-tech companies in the world which had the lowest R&D investments as percentage of sales − just 3.2 percent. And yet the senior executives in BCG's survey still considered it the world's most innovative company in 2006, 2007 and 2008. There are considerable differences in companies' abilities to benefit from their innovation investments. Let's look at the value Nordic companies get from their investments. The following is a list of 20 companies' R&D investments in percentage of sales compared to profit margin.

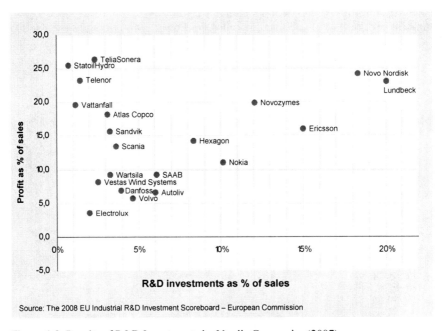

Source: The 2008 EU Industrial R&D Investment Scoreboard – European Commission

Figure 1.3. Results of R&D Investments by Nordic Companies (2007)

The graph of the 20 companies is in the shape of a 'y'. You can faintly see a correlation by looking at the axis starting at Electrolux and moving to the right through production companies like Danfoss, Volvo and SAAB, past high-tech companies like Hexagon, Nokia and Ericsson. In the right-hand corner, you find the companies that spend the most on R&D, but also those with the largest profit margins: the pharmaceutical companies Novozymes, Novo Nordisk and Lundbeck. But many companies manage to achieve large profit margins despite more modest R&D investments, including, in particular, energy companies and telecom companies. This suggests that the correlation between profitability and

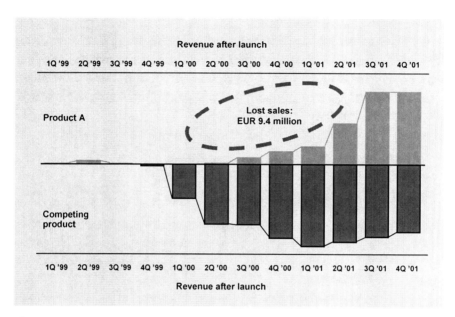

Figure 1.4. Lost Earnings Due to Slow Innovation

R&D investments is sector-specific. However, obviously, it is not possible, based on this simple analysis, to conclude that large-scale R&D investments generally lead to large profit margins.

We would like to illustrate how efficient innovation processes can influence business creation with an example involving two competing companies. The example comes from our work with one of the two companies. The above figure shows the two companies' revenue on a comparable product during the launch phase.

The first company launched product A in early 1999, but communication problems arose between the development department and sales, and the product experienced technical problems. The sales department was not prepared to take over the product because they had bad experiences trusting the development plans they received. Consequently, the finished product lay on the shelf for six months waiting for the sales staff to be trained.

Unfortunately, the product became known in the market and a competitor exploited the situation by quickly developing and launching a competing product. They soon captured a good share of the market, and after a year, the company with the original idea experienced at least EUR 10 million in lost revenue.

The competitor's fast reaction time was impressive. This example supports the assumption that fast processes within a company result in a strategic agility, which is valuable in a highly competitive market. In innovation, more than anywhere else in the company, "time is money".

So How Do We Get Better?

All arguments support a stronger effort in relation to improving the innovation process. Another reason there is so much to be gained by improving innovation processes in companies is that we are dealing with an extremely difficult task. The two main challenges are:

- Difficulty knowing what has the highest effect
- Difficulty making and maintaining improvements

Difficulty Knowing What Has the Highest Effect

What improves the innovation processes most: A creativity course for the employees or training in customer feedback methods on a specific innovation project? Even though this is a little question, it is difficult to answer. So what about the big questions?

The decision to initiate improvements and fundamentally change the way you innovate and develop your business requires intuition, experience and a very good understanding of the nature of innovation work. And often there are no data-supported analyses to show you exactly where to start.

Difficulty Making and Maintaining Improvements

An innovation environment or project is a complex entity that spans across many different functions, disciplines, career dreams, partner companies and user groups. It is much more difficult to have a fast impact on the bottom line with improvements here than it is in a production environment. This is because the human factor plays a much bigger role in innovation.

The most important assets:
- Production: materials, equipment and processes
- Innovation: people, knowledge and relations

People are also key resources in some production processes, but within innovation, people and relations are practically all there is.

The difficulty of making improvements can be illustrated with the following example. Many companies have tried to get the company's functions to work together using 'integrated product development'. Even though everyone recognizes the need for an integrated approach, it is difficult to transfer it from the innovation manual to real life. In some companies, for instance, the marketing department is officially represented in a development project, but does not actually contribute to the project. They do not have time to participate in the project work, and instead wait to get involved until the developers have a final solution. But the whole point of integrated development is that all relevant functions help shape the product together, and this requires new thinking on behalf of both the marketing and development staff.

Innovation processes primarily take place within the minds of the employees, which makes them the key to success when it comes to improvement initiatives. Developing employee competencies is therefore a crucial part of streamlining knowledge work.

Lean Innovation as a Framework for Improvement

Lean innovation is a possible answer to the question: "How can our innovation processes be more efficient?" If we move high enough up the hierarchy of objectives, all improvement initiatives have the same objective. So it is tempting to claim that lean innovation offers nothing new. This is not the first time in history that people have focused on improving the speed of innovation. The fundamental focus – the substance – is the same, namely knowledge and learning and prioritization processes. So what's new?

As an approach to a process that creates improved performance, lean innovation has a number of special strengths. Lean innovation is a management philosophy and a terminology for continuous improvements, but it is also a set of specific methods for knowledge-sharing and management. Lean innovation is 'hard' and uncompromising in its demand for focus and progress, but 'soft' and appreciative when it comes to commitment and learning. And lean innovation has a direct impact on the challenges that global senior executives face in the innovation area.

The solutions that lean advocates are 'low-tech – high-touch'. This means you choose the simplest solutions, which may not be very technically advanced, but which establish a closeness and commitment when used, and which meet the need completely. For example, Ramboll Oil & Gas successfully planned a design project for a floating oil production vessel using Post-its on a board.

In many ways, lean moves against the current when it comes to what you commonly see when improving innovation work. It introduces simple standards rather than allowing everyone to invent their own systems. When communicating, for instance, you use what you already have produced instead of creating elegant presentations aimed only at the management team.

The above examples are not exhaustive descriptions of lean innovation, but examples of the changes lean innovation can result in.

Motivation for Lean in Companies

The present century was only a few days old when a number of Scandinavian companies started showing an interest in lean innovation. They dared to embrace the apparent paradox between lean and innovation, between predictability and creativity. Why did they do it?

Coloplast, a manufacturer of health care products, began implementing lean innovation in 2003 based on very positive lean results from the production area. Their theory was that successful lean principles from production – such as 'customer value', 'flow' and 'continuous improvements' – could also create value in product development. Even as an innovative company, they believed there was room for improvement. Coloplast started with lean innovation in the development department of the Ostomy Care Division. The objective was to test different tools to get specific experience in their use and results – it was an experiment.

After learning as much as possible in one business area, lean innovation was subsequently implemented in all business areas in connection with a corporate-level lean initiative.

Now let's leave health care products and go off-shore to the North Sea between Denmark and the UK. There, Maersk's, Statoil's and Hydro's oil platforms operate in all kinds of weather to produce the oil and gas that has made Norway one of the richest countries in the world and made Denmark self-sufficient when it comes to energy. One of the companies that helps keep production running smoothly is Ramboll Oil & Gas. Ramboll is an engineering consulting firm that delivers complex solutions in "paper form". Ramboll has defined an ambitious growth plan, focusing on new markets, larger projects and increased earnings. The plan requires innovative thinking about cooperation across departments, offices and regions. The head of the lean initiative, Anders Rødgaard Knudsen, explains: "We had a feeling that something needed to change."

Ramboll initiated the lean process in the hopes it would enable them to make significant evolutionary changes without "pulling everything apart". In more revolutionary approaches to change – such as BPR (Business Process Reengineering) from the 1990s – there is a kind of non-acceptance of what you have done in the past. "And that was absolutely not the signal we wanted to send," says Anders Rødgaard Knudsen. Ramboll started lean innovation with two central questions:

- What can we do better in a customer-oriented project process like ours?
- How can we initiate improvements that are driven by our engineers and not just by management? How can we start an employee-driven evolution?

Furthermore, these challenges also had to be addressed without "destroying" things that worked well.

LINAK, the world's largest manufacturer of linear actuators, has a different story. LINAK had experienced a flood of business opportunities and had a technology that was well-suited for use in more market segments. After working with lean in production and achieving good results, they were inspired to find out if other areas in the company could benefit from a similar improvement process. They chose, among others, the development department because the management team felt they kept hiring more employees without producing more products. Working together, management defined five objectives for lean innovation:

- Greater accuracy on milestones and results
- More projects completed with the same resources
- Reduced project time
- Better balance in the portfolio between customer, technology and platform projects
- Greater predictability, including ability to keep agreements

LINAK was also highly motivated by a growth ambition that required more innovation power. This need was not being met even though they hired more and more people. The development department was extremely focused on short-term obligations and product modifications in the existing portfolio, so they did not have the energy to support the growth strategy.

Many other Nordic companies have also worked with lean innovation for several years. Scania, Danfoss, LEGO, Autoliv, Nordea Life & Pension, Arla Foods and Novo Nordisk have all begun developing their innovation processes based on lean. And when you ask these companies why, they almost always say two things:

- They want to spread the lean successes from production to development and the rest of the firm. Many companies have made the lean principles their fundamental way of thinking. They want to create a 'Lean Enterprise'.
- They want to benefit more from their significant investments in R&D. They want to increase their speed and their ability to respond in the innovation system, but also to establish a system for increasing value creation from products to services.

The Second Toyota Paradox and Lean Innovation

In 1995, MIT professor Allen Ward published a study entitled "The Second Toyota Paradox: How Delaying Decisions Can Make Better Cars Faster". Throughout the 1990s, he and several colleagues studied Toyota's R&D method. Before he began, the Toyota Production System (TPS) was widely recognized and had formed the basis for what we call lean production in the Western world. And it had been demonstrated that lean made Toyota much better at production than other automotive manufacturers.

The question Ward asked was whether Toyota was also better at developing products and services than its competitors.

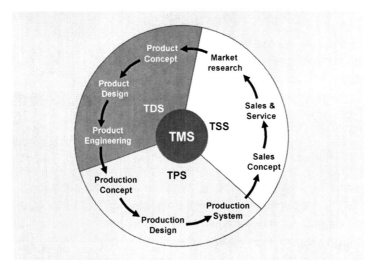

Figure 1.5. Toyota Development System (TDS) as Part of the Complete Toyota Management System (TMS)

Allen Ward discovered that Toyota was extremely efficient, also when it came to innovation. Like TPS, Toyota also had TDS (Toyota Development System). Together with their Sales System, they were all part of an overall Management System (TMS). He learned that Toyota's development engineers were dedicated to working with continuous improvements, i.e. they went to the root of the problem based on the logic that all big problems start out as small problems. They used Visual Planning & Management (or what is referred to in lean terminology using the Japanese word *oobeya*). For example, the development engineers gathered together their experiences visually, in the form of drawings, diagrams and tables, in a personal handbook. This made it easier to quickly and efficiently share their knowledge with others. This is similar to the portfolios that creative people in architecture, advertising and art use to show the world what they have mastered and experienced.

Toyota gave the technical experts (knowledge workers) a surprising amount of freedom to create solutions. The project manager on a given innovation project, for example developing a new Corolla, was responsible for everything relating to the development of that new vehicle. There were no noticeable conflicts with the line managers. The project manager was 'director' of the new Corolla, and everyone knew it.

Allen Ward also found out that Toyota had a specific competency when it came to working with several parallel solution concepts at the same time. In an innovation project, for example, they would develop in parallel three different concepts for engine mounts. Only then were they ready to choose the type of mount that would be most suitable for the car model in question. A very typical problem in innovation processes is that you have to make a number of crucial decisions at the start of the process even though you do not actually have enough information to make good decisions. Toyota avoided this problem with parallel development and by postponing important decisions until enough insight had been generated.

Just like the Toyota Production System has become lean production in the West, the Toyota Development System is the father of what we call lean innovation. And like Womack and Jones did within production, Allen Ward studied Toyota's competencies within innovation. Unfortunately, Ward did not have the chance to make the concept of lean innovation stick in the same way Womack and Jones did with lean production. In 2004, Allen Ward died in a plane crash. He was flying an airplane he had designed himself. He died a dedicated innovator.

The Impact of Lean Innovation in Scandinavia – and in Japan

We have asked our case companies about the effect of lean innovation, and they point to both measurable and non-measurable effects.

At Coloplast, working with lean has resulted in people thinking more about how they work with their development projects and calling attention to obstacles in the development work. Today, the lead time on a development project is reduced, and projects are completed in just six months without having a negative effect on the energy or creativity of the staff – on the contrary.

Exhausto has worked with lean innovation since 2006. They have developed a common language for talking about improvements in production and development. And the management team has worked to obtain a much better idea of the key success factors in the innovation process.

Lean has had a notable effect within four areas:

- Increased product quality as a result of continuous follow-up on quality, both during and after development.
- Better accuracy when it comes to customer needs through increased dialog with customers and sales before initiating development.
- Less rework through parallel work with alternative concepts.
- Less stress on key resources and specialists with the help of two-week visual resource planning.

With lean innovation, LINAK has managed to establish more integration in the development work. The different functions contribute more and have a better understanding of their role in the innovation process. They are now much more conscious of the development process, important milestones and visual processes. Lean has contributed to greater accuracy in project completion. Implementing lean has increased product quality and user-friendliness by involving the customers in a new way. The products have become more 'right'. Project ownership, visibility and focus has improved considerably.

At Ramboll Oil & Gas, everyone in top management agrees that the company has benefited significantly from the introduction of lean. The customers have noticed the new and improved working methods, which is a very significant result.

Ramboll's most important results are:

- Better and faster start-up of innovation projects by working consciously to increase the knowledge level in the beginning.
- A common improvement language at management level and greater focus on customer value.
- Increased job satisfaction among employees thanks to structured visual communication and precisely defined deliverables and deadlines.

ECCO is also satisfied with the implementation of lean innovation. Along with improved interaction between the projects and support, it has resulted in a clearer project organization around the different product segments, resulting in better use of resources. In their evaluations, the employees primarily emphasize the soft results, saying that lean innovation has resulted in: better communication, greater overview, better general understanding and better project flow.

The hard results in the form of measurable performance is an area ECCO is continuing to work on. According to ECCO, one of the challenges with lean is that you have to get used to measuring performance in the innovation environment. This is a cultural change and it takes time.

But let's return to Japan and Allen Ward's question. Was Toyota also better than its competitors when it came to innovation?

Yes! On key innovation parameters, Toyota was better than both European and North American automotive manufacturers. They were two to three times faster at developing new car models. They developed five times as many prototypes and consumed only half as many resources developing a new car model.

But if you aren't a developer for an automotive manufacturer and you prefer Ferrari to Toyota, can you actually use this information for anything?

Top 15 most innovative companies	2008 ranking
Apple, USA	1
Google, USA	2
Toyota Motor, Japan	3
General Electric Company, USA	4
Microsoft Corporation, USA	5
Tata Group, India	6
Nintendo, Japan	7
Procter & Gamble, USA	8
Sony Corporation	9
Nokia Corporation, Finland	10
Amazon.com, USA	11
IBM Corporation, USA	12
Research In Motion, Canada	13
BMW Group, Germany	14
Hewlett-Packard Company, USA	15

Source: BCG 2008 Senior Executive Innovation Survey

Figure 1.6. The 15 Most Innovative Companies in the World

We think you can. First, Toyota has generated profits for 30 years in a row, and is today the world's largest automotive manufacturer. Second, and just as interesting, in 2008, the 3,000 global senior executives ranked Toyota the third most innovative company in the world after Apple and Google.

Literature:

Boston Consulting Group: "Innovation 2008 – is the Tide Turning? – A BCG Senior Management Survey".

Doz, Yves & Kosonen, Mikko: *Fast Strategy*. Wharton School Publishing, 2008.

Liker, Jeffrey K.: *The Toyota Way*. McGraw Hill, 2004.

The 2008 EU Industrial R&D Investment Scoreboard – European Commission – 2008.

Ward, Allen, John J. Christiano, Jeffrey K. Liker & Durward K. Sobek: "The Second Toyota Paradox: How Delaying Decisions Can Make Better Cars Faster". *Sloan Management Review*, Spring 1995.

Ward, Allen, Jeffrey K. Liker & Durward K. Sobek : "Another Look at How Toyota Integrates Product Development", *Harvard Business Review*. July 1, 1998.

Womack, James P., Daniel T. Jones & Daniel Ross: *The Machine that Changed the World*. Macmillan Publishing.

Womack, James P. & Daniel T. Jones: *Lean Thinking*. Simon & Schuster, 1996.

Worthen, Ben: "Innovation Comes Cheap At Apple", Blog, *Wall Street Journal*, 2008.

Part II
Understanding the Fundamentals

Chapter 2
Understanding Innovation

Innovation has been a subject of scientific research for many years, and you can find a lot of valuable information for use in your effort to streamline the innovation process. In this chapter, we will discuss what innovation is and which mechanisms work in the innovation process. We will concentrate specifically on the type of innovation that takes place in large knowledge-based organizations.

Defining Innovation

Innovation is an exceedingly popular subject. At the time of going to press, googling the word 'innovation' produced around 92,100,000 hits. And should the reader try now, chances are the number of hits has increased. Innovation is a very positive term and is particularly popular in business. Often we also see the term used to make discussions, power-points and solutions appear more interesting and visionary.

There are many good definitions of innovation, and there is quite a lot of variation. Some define innovation simply as the process of introducing something new, while to others, innovation must be patentable.

Innovation = The introduction of a new product or service in the market or of a product or service with significantly improved features (OECD)

Innovation = Something new that has a value in the market (The EU Innovation Council)

Innovation = Insight + ideas + impact (?WhatIf! The Innovation Company)

Innovation = New and useful (Ours)

Figure 2.1. Definitions of Innovation

According to most definitions, innovation must be new and value-creating. Consequently, innovation is a creative idea that has been implemented. We usually say that innovation is something that is both 'new and useful'.

C. Sehested, H. Sonnenberg, *Lean Innovation,* DOI 10.1007/978-3-642-15895-7_3,
© Springer-Verlag Berlin Heidelberg 2011

The fundamental element of innovation is that it contains something that has never been seen before. Something that has been done in an entirely new way. However, it can be difficult to define exactly how new this 'something' must be, which is where the idea of 'patentability' comes in. It can either be incremental or radical in nature. Most innovation is incremental, comprising improvements on previous solutions which may not immediately seem pioneering in themselves. Other key dimensions are novelty value in relation to technology, the markets and internal or external conditions. We believe the most important perspective is that of the recipient, because it is generally the recipient, i.e. the customer, who determines whether something is sufficiently novel to make it a true innovation.

One example of an innovation is the Apple iPod, which has taken the world by storm. From a technological point of view, you could argue that the product is not an innovation: it's 'just' a digital walkman. But according to customers, it is an amazing and ingenious product, and that is what makes the iPod an innovation.

Our definition of innovation includes a dimension of 'usefulness'. The novelty must be useful and, thus, value-creating. This usefulness can be generated in two ways – either by simplifying the solution's production process or by creating more value for the customer. Here, too, we believe that value must be assessed primarily from the point of view of the recipient. The recipient may be the patient, the user, the customer or anyone else who benefits from the innovation. The central themes of value creation and implementation distinguish creative ideas, new approaches or discoveries from true innovation. New ideas that are not implemented and do not create value are not innovations.

Businesses can benefit from being innovative in more than one area. The most successful businesses have all achieved success by being innovative in one or more of the following four areas:

- Business structures
- Core and support processes
- Products and services
- Supply and distribution set-up

In practice, the innovation process can be made more interesting and successful by widening the focus slightly and by operating with a broader understanding of the concept of innovation. We have seen projects derail because the people involved felt they couldn't improve on the physical product, and they only got back on track once everyone took a broader approach to innovation.

The Challenge of Innovation

The challenge faced when working with innovation has been put into words nicely by J.C. Jones in his book *Design Methods*:

> *"The fundamental problem is that designers are obliged to use current information to predict a future state that will not come about unless their predictions are correct. The final outcome of designing has to be assumed before the means of achieving it can be explored: the designers have to work backwards in time from an assumed effect upon the world to the beginning of a chain of events that will bring the effect about."*

Innovation is a very complex challenge, requiring a good imagination and involving many risk elements. Innovation is a learning process that requires a great deal of trial and error.

Creating something new is a process of synthesis in contrast to analysis, which is the process of taking things apart. Synthesis is not just something engineers do when designing new machines or products. Plenty of development work takes place within other professions, such as medicine, law, trade and architecture. The intellectual activity that creates new products is no different to that used when advising a sick patient, drawing up a sales plan or developing a social plan for a local authority.

It is strange that universities provide so little training in synthesis, despite the fact that it is at the heart of many professions. Herbert A. Simon, a scientist famed for his work in artificial intelligence, is quite critical of the educational system. He primarily blames universities for placing more emphasis on the analytical disciplines rather than teaching people how to work with synthesis. Critical analytical thinking and decomposition are considered more worthwhile pursuits than using your know-how and creativity to create something new. We see the results of the teaching practices and attitudes that have been forced on people on practically a daily basis. People may be very good at what they do, and they may be very knowledgeable, but they face huge challenges when called upon to bring this knowledge into play in the process of creating something new. Many would benefit from focusing less on analytical critical thinking and finding weak points in other people's ideas and, instead, view them as a source of inspiration that can be built on.

In the innovation process, there is clearly a need to understand what happens when we work together to create something new. This is true at manager level, where the conditions for the innovation process are set, but also at employee level. The potential for efficiency in the innovation process is not so much that it generates more creative ideas or more individual professional competencies.

Rather, it is because it increases the quality and speed of the processes that produce ideas based on the interaction of many people.

Innovation as a Team Effort

"Enlightened trial and error succeeds over the planning of the lone genius."
Tom Kelly, IDEO

In the minds of many, the word innovation produces an image of the introverted genius working alone to come up with a radical new solution to a huge problem. But that is a rare situation, indeed.

In innovation discussions, you often hear the story about how Art Fry at 3M was developing a new type of glue that accidentally turned out not to be sticky enough. And presto, he had invented the Post-it. However, most innovations require the coordinated efforts of a lot of people. And you can be sure that 3M used the persevering innovation work of many people to create the business success that the Post-it ultimately became.

Danfoss Drives, a manufacturer of frequency converters, once developed a new product that became a major success for the company. Out of gratitude for their hard work, the management wanted to reward everyone who had contributed to the development of the product with a box of chocolates. They thought they would need about 20 or 30 boxes. Then the project manager began to draw up a list of everyone involved and thus deserving of recognition. This turned out to be harder than they originally thought. Everyone was surprised when the list of people who had contributed to the project from idea to launch grew to more than 100 names.

Both examples show that innovation in large knowledge-based organizations is not about what one person can do, but about what the organization can do based on the coordinated efforts of many dedicated people. To innovate better, you need to understand how these processes work. You need to think about what promotes team learning and what hinders it.

Team Learning and Prioritization

The way we organize ourselves around an innovation project should support the processes that need to take place between the participants so they can make the most of their own and each other's competencies. This may sound simple, but in reality very few manage to create a setting that effectively promotes the innovation process. The key to a successful innovation environment is under-standing which processes to support.

Innovation is a team learning and prioritization process. In order to work with these processes, you need to understand that team learning is based on individual learning. It is possible that two people can have the same experi-ences and learn in the same way, but the actual act of learning takes place within the individual participant. Thus, team learning is based on the experiences and reflections of the individual.

To transform individual learning into team learning, a process needs to take place in which the individual shares his or her knowledge with the other mem-bers of the team. The team can, then, interpret what they have learned, integrate it and raise it to a new level of shared knowledge. To do this, they need to be in regular contact, have discussions and compare their own experiences with those of their team members. This new shared knowledge will subsequently form the foundation for the actions of both the individual and the team. Team learning, thus, comprises three steps:

- Individual learning
- Knowledge-sharing with the team
- Interpretation and integration within the team

The three steps of team learning play an important role in achieving efficient innovation. It is a bad idea for the team to focus too much on individual learning at the expense of knowledge-sharing and the subsequent interpreting process. To achieve team learning, you need to dedicate sufficient time and space in the process. It is not uncommon for project participants to hold too few meetings because they prioritize their own individual learning too highly. They forget that they are not working alone on the project and that they are supposed to be helping each other learn more across disciplines and functions. Value is created by sharing knowledge about the possibilities and limitations and by working together to find new solutions.

Team meetings are often given lower priority because the knowledge-shar-ing and team learning process is poorly organized. This can result in the gen-eral view that the meetings are a waste of time. However, this problem can be solved. If the participants always bear in mind the purpose of their meetings – knowledge-sharing, interpretation and activation – it is possible to organize the meetings better and thus make participation more attractive.

A few years ago, we had an interesting experience working with a biochemical company. A project team under serious time pressure was trying to figure out how they could speed up a research project.

The team comprised highly trained specialists from several different disciplines. Their cooperation was not optimal because they were having a hard time planning meetings, and as specialists they were not used to interdisciplinary project work. The participants had filled their calendars with individual project-related activities that couldn't be rescheduled. When we took a closer look at their calendars, they turned out to be booked with lab experiments, data analyses, meetings with international researchers and conferences all over the world. The team came to the conclusion that the project could be accelerated if they worked together in one room and if they held more frequent status meetings within the team. This would increase focus on the assignment, and thus increase the level of team learning and speed up the process.

It was a good and clear-cut solution, but the participants did not think it was feasible. They claimed there was no tradition for several disciplines working together in one room. Moreover, they believed they lacked the necessary facilities and were concerned that they would not be able to work efficiently on such heavy problems in that kind of environment because of noise and disruptions. Consequently, they decided to stick to the status quo. This is a classic example of how difficult it can be to change firmly established working patterns, to try something new, to be curious and develop new ways of working together rather than only concentrating on one's own specialization – and this actually happened in a development department!

Culture and Physical Environment

"Culture is the software of the mind." Geert Hofstede

The results of an innovation project depend on both the individual and the team performance. To achieve efficient innovation, we need to look at both how the individual works and how the team members work together. The culture that exists within the organization has a significant impact on efficiency. It can both strengthen and impede efficiency – and here we need to remember that there are two dimensions: good solutions and good processes. When we talk about organizational culture, we mean a pattern of shared fundamental assumptions about the correct way to perceive, think and feel. These assumptions form the basis for how managers perceive and perform their managerial responsibilities, and they have a major influence on how employees behave.

You can find out how a specific corporate culture works by answering the following questions: What kind of relationship do you have with customers and other key stakeholders? Is it okay to contact them directly to initiate a dialog, even when you are uncertain, or would that be considered a sign of weakness? Is the individual employee a responsible, independent person who thinks for him or herself, or is he or she simply expected to obey orders? Is there an interest in development and improvement or does there seem to be a preference for the status quo?

The organizational culture is closely tied to how success is viewed within the organization. What does the management focus on, and what direction do the decisions point in? What is required and considered important? Working consciously with the culture is an important aspect of improving a company's innovation process. But the culture is also one of the hardest things to change. There are, however, other more tangible areas where changes can be more easily made to improve the innovation process:

The organizational and decision-making structure is reflected in the people who have been hired, in how they are grouped together and in how decisions are made within the organization. It is about assignments, responsibilities and staffing, as well as linking strategy, tactics and operational decisions.

The measurement and incentive system comprises the strategies, goals, sub-goals and operational performance targets that have been set. It also covers the incentives and recognition for achieving goals and targets. But the most important element may be what the goals express in terms of ambitions for productivity, readiness and impact.

Processes and methods represents the sum of the processes, methods and tools used in the innovation process. They also include how knowledge is gathered and utilized within the company. Examples of methods and tools are project models, process descriptions, IT tools and lab procedures.

The physical framework is the physical environment viewed in relation to the innovation process.

If the marketing department and the development department are located far from each other, team learning can be difficult. Establishing the right physical conditions means bringing the participants in the innovation process closer together.

Open and Closed Problems

Now, let's take a closer look at the area of processes and methods, which is key to establishing efficiency and predictability in the innovation process.

Problem-solving is a crucial element in the innovation process. Often, a 'problem' is considered negative but in innovation it is neutral. Our definition of a problem is something that arises when a problem solver decides to fulfill a need by finding a solution. There are different types of problems, and whether we have 'understood' the problem correctly plays a key role in how efficiently it is solved.

There is a tendency to underestimate problems and to attempt to solve them using methods that are not ideal. This often means doing things that were not originally intended, thus increasing both time and resource consumption. Even though this may all take place at micro level, it can still disrupt the speed, predictability and efficiency of an innovation project. Generally speaking, there are two types of problems: open and closed. Closed problems have only one solution and can often be solved mathematically or logically. Open problems have more than one solution.

Closed problems	Open problems
Jigsaw puzzles	Social development
Accounting	Development product
Measuring distance	New manufacturing process
Quadratic equation	Traffic planning
Taking inventory	Market launch

Figure 2.2. Examples of Closed and Open Problems

If you are dealing with an open problem, but can only see one solution, it is often a good idea to force yourself to find several alternatives before deciding on a specific solution. Otherwise how would you know that you have identified the best solution? One approach is to work on several potential solutions at the same time and then have the 'solutions' compete against each other.

Working with alternatives can reduce development time because it speeds up the learning process and gives you something to fall back on if a solution turns out to be unworkable. During the process, however, it can often be difficult to treat alternatives equally. Developers have a tendency to fall in love with one of the potential solutions at too early a stage. Learning to define equivalent potential solutions and treat them all objectively takes practice.

Prioritization and Solution Selection

More than anything else, problem-solving is a question of prioritization and decision-making. Because making such a decision can be a rather complex process, it can be helpful to work with the concept of a 'solution space'. A solution space contains every acceptable solution, and for open problems it will contain several potential solutions. In order to select the most optimum solution, you need to carry out a more detailed evaluation, defining criteria, performing any physical tests and taking account of customers' ideas. That is why developing criteria for the solution in the form of requirements and wishes is an integral part of the problem-solving and innovation process.

Visualization

Visualization is a highly effective and necessary part of any problem-solving process. In fact, describing an idea in words, in a drawing or in an illustration helps increase the problem-solver's intelligence. Visualization also improves communication, both internally within the innovation team and externally. Communication in writing and drawings is part of the problem-solver's toolbox. In some cases, it can be helpful to speak in images or develop a special language for use during the problem-solving process. The design firm IDEO gives an example from a project they worked on with a toothpaste manufacturer. The assignment was to develop a new type of packaging, and the project team ended up developing an entirely new language about toothpaste during the problem-solving process to help them verbalize how the toothpaste flowed out of the tube and how it felt to squeeze the tube.

Wicked Problems

A special type of open problem is 'wicked' problems, which are the most complex of all problems. Wicked problems were first described in connection with social planning and they are characterized by the fact that they change constantly. Just when you think you have found a solution and you begin to implement it, you impact the situation, it changes and you have to start over.

Take, for example, a problem from the world of traffic planning: how to increase the capacity of a specific stretch of freeway. This can be done by adding more lanes. However, that makes it more attractive for people to travel by car, thus causing an increase in traffic volume. And that increase ultimately leads to more complaints about noise, increased congestion on the on and off-ramps and parking problems. So, while the original problem is solved, the solution creates a series of new problems. Similarly complex problems are often seen within politics and legislation.

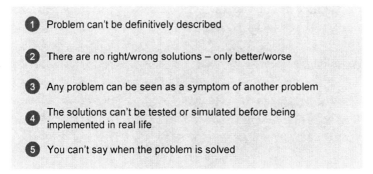

Figure 2.3. Five Characteristics of Wicked Problems

We have introduced the theory of wicked problems here because such complex problems represent an extreme in the world of problem-solving. We often see people trying to solve problems using methods that are too simple. The problem-solving methods for wicked problems can serve as inspiration for the efficient solution of other complex problems, thus, helping increase predictability in the problem-solving process. To increase the efficiency of the process of solving complex problems, it is important to bear the following in mind:

1. No single individual possesses the knowledge needed to solve the problem. And the biggest experts are most often the prospective users of the solution.
2. No one wants to be subjected to other people's plans without being involved in the process.
3. Decisions are not based only on professional expertise. They are often also political, moral or ethical in nature.
4. The problem-solver's role is to facilitate the process rather than propose solutions.
5. You can not predict all possible consequences of a solution – any potential solution is a journey involving an unknown number of risks along the way.

Looking at how to deal with wicked problems can be very inspiring in the innovation process. For instance, you can involve the customers in the development process to let them know that you understand that their needs may change once they see the solution. You can also view your role as that of a facilitator who promotes the solution of complex problems through a negotiation-oriented process.

Many inexperienced project managers have a tendency to take too simplistic a view of problems. They do not see their complexity, and end up selecting a problem-solving process that is too simple, thus causing delays and turbulence. But not all problems are complex, and applying problem-solving methods for wicked problems to simple problems can prove a wasteful approach. That is why it is important to develop the skills and experience to be able to evaluate problems correctly and to alternate between different problem-solving methods as needed.

Structure of the Innovation Process

The following figure illustrates an innovation process organized in the form of a project comprising a series of processes, each of which consists of different working methods.

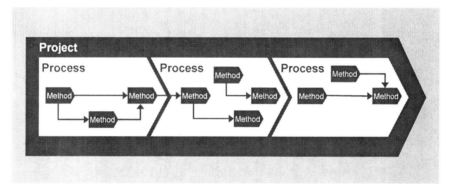

Figure 2.4. The Innovation Process

If you want to work efficiently, it is important to constantly question the processes and methods used in projects. They need to be developed and optimized, and it is a good idea to collect helpful process elements for use in connection with future innovation projects. In much the same way as a handyman is equipped with a toolbox, the knowledge worker should also have newly sharpened and well-maintained tools in his or her box.

Innovation with Extreme Concepts

Now we would like to present an innovation process from our toolbox. This process is intended for use in the early phases of a project to generate a large number of ideas and establish a stable foundation for the later phases. The

process spans from idea, through alternative concepts, to a final realistic solution. We call the process Innovation with Extreme Concepts.

To illustrate the process, let's look at an example from a hospital where
the management initiated a project to improve the service level in the hospital
emergency room. There had been a negative atmosphere among the ER staff
for some time. In addition, the management had been repeatedly confronted by
stories from patients and politicians about the low quality of the service, so they
decided to launch a project to design the 'ER of the Future'.

To carry out the project, an interdisciplinary team was appointed, comprising a wide range of professional competencies. Initially, the assignment was to
present two or three alternative solutions for how to improve the ER.

The project team followed the process illustrated in Figure 2.5. The model
comprises three phases, with the first phase – the 'needs and ideas phase' – consisting of gathering information about user needs. The first phase produces three
significant results:

- An understanding of the problem
- Requirements and wishes for the solution
- A collection of initial ideas

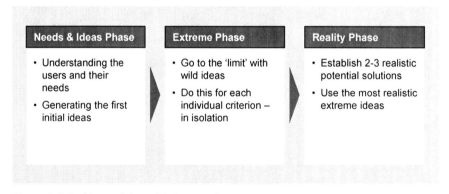

Figure 2.5. Problem-solving with Extreme Concepts

The project team identified the stakeholders and visited the ER to talk to staff
and patients. The policy-makers visited the hospital, and the legislation was
reviewed. During the visit to the ER, photos were taken and videos were made.
The staff collected quantitative data and participated in focus groups to talk
about the current strengths and possibilities. While all this information was being
gathered, ideas for how the ER could be improved were captured on an ongoing basis. They might be little ideas based on an individual patient's experience

or ideas the staff had been talking about for a long time. The project team collected and documented these ideas. At the same time, the project team analyzed the interviews and drew conclusions based on the stakeholders' requirements and wishes. They were added to a list which was regularly questioned and re-evaluated.

The next phase was the 'extreme phase'. The most significant outcome of this phase was generating a number of 'wild' ideas and listing solutions that were optimized to comply with only a single criterion. This phase was used to generate as many ideas as possible without worrying about the fact that the final solution needed to comply with a whole set of criteria. The project team, then, combined the ideas into a number of complete solutions.

In the ER example, the project team finally decided on four extreme criteria for a solution: high level of medical expertise, good care, short waiting times and low price. The project team conducted a workshop with the ER staff, where 'wild' ideas were generated for each criterion without considering the other criteria. For example, the team came up with the following extreme ideas for the high level of medical expertise criterion: fly in leading experts for every single treatment; set up video conference facilities in the operating room to obtain fast second opinions; and establish permanent treatment teams that train difficult situations in a simulator. Obviously, these ideas were unrealistic in their current form, but they helped widen the range of possible solutions. This made way for creativity and for exploring the different possible solutions. In innovation, there is a fine line between an ingenious solution and a crazy solution.

The final phase was the 'reality phase'. In this phase, work continued on the ideas from the previous two phases, only they were adjusted to meet a realistic and balanced set of criteria. This means dropping some of the 'wild' ideas and replacing them with more feasible ones. This phase will typically produce one to three final solution proposals which will then form the basis for selecting the final solution.

In the ER example, the team proposed addressing 'lack of medical expertise' by compiling a phone list of leading experts, introducing telemedicine facilities and training in permanent teams.

Analysis of 'Innovation with Extreme Concepts'

The example above is an excellent illustration of how an innovation project can be designed to integrate many useful elements in an efficient innovation process. In the following, we will pull out and describe the elements which have consciously been built into the process to increase the degree of innovation and realism of the final solution.

An understanding of user needs is obtained in a simple manner through personal observation and by visiting the ER to speak with people who are affected by the problem. Problem-solvers often tend to base their solutions only on information received from others, and it's not uncommon to find more than three links between those with the need and the problem-solver.

Knowledge and ideas are gathered continuously, not only at the end. During the initial visits, the team collects user ideas, which form the basis for preliminary outlines of ideas. It is important to establish an interaction between analysis and synthesis throughout the innovation process. If, at the end of the process, all you have is a lot of raw data, it can be nearly impossible to draw conclusions and create a final solution.

The best way to solve big problems is to break them down into smaller problems. By breaking down 'Good patient service' into the four sub-problems of medical expertise, care, waiting times and price, the task becomes more manageable.

Structure helps heighten creativity. It is very difficult to come up with good ideas without constraints, and it can be stimulating to take a simple problem or a single criterion as a point of departure. Within every criterion, there is room in the extreme phase of the process for crazy ideas and for experimentation. When working in a team, it can be a good idea to agree on when creativity should be let loose and when it should be limited. We find that the system works best if creativity is allowed to flow freely during the first of the three phases in the process. By that time, the work should have progressed far enough to provide a good understanding of the problem, but there should also still be time before specific solutions need to be presented.

The team works actively to interpret requirements and wishes. In the example, we see that requirements and wishes are formulated during the first phase. It makes sense to define the criteria for a solution before developing it, as this gives the work a common direction. However, this is also a somewhat idealized scenario, as the tests carried out and the accumulated knowledge and experiences gained throughout the process continuously influence the requirements and wishes. The team therefore needs to be able to work actively with the requirements and wishes not only at the beginning but throughout the process.

Prototyping solutions quickly provides useful insights. In the reality phase, the team tested several solutions by discussing them with nurses and other stakeholders. During a development process, it is important to find out what happens when ideas meet reality. This is because of the nature of open problems and the need for user response, but also because prototyping helps the developer visualize the real-life situation where the solution must work.

Planning and implementing prototypes and simulations can be quite resource-demanding, and we often see prototyping that is incomplete or carried out too late in the process. One reason for this is that the project team can be so focused on developing and presenting the complete solution that they simply do not have the time or energy to test ideas. Testing can start to feel like a disruption to the creative process. And because there is a tendency to allocate insufficient time to the first part of the project, the knowledge-generating prototyping process is often dropped to save time. However, this can have the unfortunate result of the untested solution being introduced only to be immediately recalled for improvements. The resource savings in the project's early phase are ultimately lost in a lengthy implementation phase characterized by re-work, delays and frustrations.

Another typical situation is that neither time nor resources are allocated to incorporating the improvement ideas that result from testing. This can be a deeply frustrating situation and can demotivate an entire project team. It is therefore a good idea to assume that it will be necessary to make changes after a round of tests and to include sufficient time and resources for this purpose in the project plan. The whole purpose of prototyping is to find out how the product can be improved. It is thus something of a paradox that time is not allocated to making these improvements.

Management of Innovation Processes

The ER example provides some insight into the situation of the developer. We have shown how the process proceeds in a structured way from needs, through specification to solution and testing, with the constant acquisition of new knowledge along the way. A problem can be broken down into smaller pieces, which can then be put back together and evaluated to reveal the consequences of implementing the new solution.

This process increases the understanding of user needs, the various potential solutions and how they influence each other. That understanding provides a basis for creative idea generation. Innovation tends to be associated primarily with creativity, even though that is not actually the most important part of the process. We have chosen to call innovation a process of prioritization as well because the ability to prioritize among different options is crucial. When working with open problems, there isn't enough time to test every option, so the ability to prioritize and be selective is an important part of the process. This takes both wisdom and intuition, and there must be room for opinions and interpretations. Development is not an exact science.

Parts of the innovation process are unstructured and unpredictable. This is a consequence of the complex learning process that takes place. It is vital that the project team understands and accepts the heuristic nature of the learning process, however it must not become a virtue in itself. Loose and uncontrolled activities can have a negative impact on the learning process. Learning in connection with open problems is a never-ending process. So the key is to develop a sense for when to make room for the unforeseen and when to impose more structure.

People who are not involved in the development process are often surprised by what takes place. How can it be so hard to manage? They may have proper cause for their wonder, as very few are able to consciously manage learning processes in the development area. However, anyone not involved also needs to understand that development is hard work and that problem-solving is a learning process which cannot be planned in detail.

The Personal Perspective

In the process of streamlining innovation, it is important to understand what it means to create something new. Consequently, personal experience with innovation is an important qualification. Innovation work brings out powerful feelings. Most people who have worked with innovation have felt the vulnerability that comes with presenting the solution they have worked hard on for so long.

Imagine spending a major part of your professional life becoming an expert in a specific field. You have studied for five or seven years at the university, perhaps, and then worked for ten years or more in a given field. You know the field inside and out, you know the literature, you know the professional environment. You have been presented with a problem which you have tried to solve, either alone or in collaboration with others. You know what works, and you have even played the role of reviewer on several occasions. You have been asked to come up with a solution to a problem and have worked with the problem constructively. You present the best solution you can come up with.

You make your statement for everyone to consider and criticize. Your self-image, your professional reputation, everything you have worked so hard to build up is put on display to be evaluated and criticized from every angle. You know the trade-offs that have been made and the limitations that have led to the solution. But the recipients don't know any of this, and now they and others are evaluating your work. This is an extremely vulnerable situation. Anyone who wants to reach you, needs to understand the situation you are in. They need to

have been there or to have a very good understanding of the courage and vulnerability you are showing at this moment.

How the knowledge worker responds in this situation is, of course, individual. But it is much more difficult to create something new than to criticize something someone else has created. We would therefore like to take this opportunity
to encourage everyone to show the greatest possible respect to those who dare
to stick their necks out and put themselves on the line to bring something new
into the world.

Literature:

Argyris, Chris: "Teaching Smart People How to Learn." *Harvard Business Review*, 2000.
Christensen, Clayton M.: The Innovators Dilemma – When New Technologies Cause Great
    Firms to Fail. Harvard Business School Publishing, 1997.
Christensen, Clayton M.: Disrupting Class. How Disruptive Innovation Will Change the Way
    the World Learns. McGraw Hill, 2008.
Doblin: "Ten Types of Innovation," http://www.doblin.com/AboutInno/innotypes.html
Jones, John Chris: *Design Methods*. Wiley & Sons. New York, 1970.
"Managing Google's Idea Factory". *Businessweek*, October 3, 2005.
Mayer, Marissa: "Google's Nine Points of Innovation." Google, 2007.
McKim, R. H.: *Experiences in Visual Thinking*. PWS Publishers, 1972.
Papanek, Victor: Design for the Real World – Human Ecology and Social Change. Academy
    Chicago Publishers, 1971.
Rittel, Horst & Melvin Webber: *Dilemmas in a General Theory of Planning*. Elsevier Scien-
    tific Publishing. Amsterdam.
Simon, Herbert A.: *Sciences of the Artificial*. MIT Press; 3rd edition, October 1, 1996.
?WHATIF!: Sticky Wisdom. John Wiley & Sons, 2004.

Chapter 3
Understanding Lean Innovation

When we want to give managers a better idea of what lean innovation is, we sometimes give them a little job to do. The purpose of the exercise is to learn how to assemble a Lego car. The managers are often a bit surprised at first that such a simple task can have anything to do with lean. But then they proceed to solve the task with great enthusiasm.

The team puts the car together and demonstrates that it works, which usually takes 15 minutes. Afterwards, we talk about how they would work if they had to make a living assembling Lego cars. The participants are given some time to think about what they would do in such a situation, and more importantly what they would do differently. They come up with a lot of ideas for improvements. They would sort the bricks first; tear the manual apart so they could work in parallel on different parts of the design; clear the table so they had a good work surface; practice so they were prepared; appoint a project manager to coordinate the work and keep track of time etc.

Figure 3.1. Lean Innovation Exercise

C. Sehested, H. Sonnenberg, *Lean Innovation*, DOI 10.1007/978-3-642-15895-7_4,
© Springer-Verlag Berlin Heidelberg 2011

After the discussion about improvements, we ask the participants to implement their ideas for improvements as they assemble a different car. This time, the participants generally manage to assemble the car in less than five minutes. Finally, we evaluate the process, and even though the car was assembled quickly and properly, the participants can actually still identify relevant potential improvements.

The best teams manage to build the car in 2.5 minutes. From 15 minutes to 2.5 minutes – that is a factor six improvement. When we evaluate the exercise afterwards, we talk about the aspects of the first round that resemble the real-life situation in a knowledge-based organization. Often, the similarities are many: Responsibilities and roles are not clearly defined, there are misunderstandings in communication and it is generally unclear what the task actually involves.

The point of the Lego exercise is that it is possible to make huge improvements by taking a step back and focusing on where things can be done better. This approach works for strategic initiatives, but it also works well for the smaller tasks that generally occupy most people's workdays. Another point is that the people who perform the tasks are generally the most qualified to improve on them. This is even truer for knowledge-based companies. A third point, and what is really interesting, is that 90 percent of the participants in this exercise actually say that the second round was the most fun – i.e. the round where they were most efficient.

Lean Innovation Is Getting Smart Faster

Lean innovation is all about fast and efficient learning. One way to do this is to focus on the process where the learning takes place and implement a system for continuously improving that process. In choosing to work with lean, you have chosen a corporate culture that constantly questions how things are done and makes it a priority to devote time and resources to getting better.

We can see that a company works with lean when it is legitimate to question the way the organization operates. And when it is obvious that management is close to the value-adding processes and spends time supporting the employees in the development of processes and methods. When there are routines that support and document continuous development. And when central lean terms, principles and methods are part of the common language spoken throughout the organization.

In fact, it doesn't really make sense to say "Now, we are a lean organization," because lean is not a specific state or destination. Lean is a direction – a journey. Lean is a corporate culture and a management philosophy. It is a culture and philosophy supported by principles and methods. But the methods are not all that matter. What really matters is the objective behind the methods.

The entire lean movement was started by Womack and Jones in an experiment to reveal the 'secret' behind Toyota's success. Since then, the words of Womack and Jones have been subjected to further interpretation. This has resulted in many good conclusions, but it has also resulted in some people maintaining the view that lean is nothing more than a handful of methods and tools to be implemented in a specific order. This view can threaten the long-term effects. This is the case in production environments, but it is even more so in innovation environments. Lean isn't just one thing. Lean isn't just 'The Toyota Way'. This is illustrated very well by an interesting discussion we had a few years ago.

One winter day in 2006, just before the start of the Christmas holidays, we met Takashi Tanaka in Stockholm, Sweden. He used to work at Toyota Engineering as a project manager and consultant. We were struck by his pragmatism as he talked about what lean is. During the interview, he explained, among other things, that Toyota had learned from its own experiences and changed its practices concerning some of the things described so thoroughly in management literature. He also encouraged us to study Honda, saying they were very clever and had achieved good results.

The meeting with Tanaka shows the strength of the inspiration Toyota can provide. It is the ability to think about what you are doing and constantly develop your methods and processes. Through humility and appreciation of the work of others, you just might find the key to your challenges. This is powerful stuff. Perhaps Toyota isn't the best source of inspiration in this particular instance. After all, Toyota has worked with lean for 60 years and manufactures cars. The concepts and methods employed should be determined by the maturity of the individual organization and the nature of its processes.

We sometimes meet people who say that lean doesn't have anything new to offer – but what organization can actually claim not to be interested in getting better? Others are disappointed when they see the lean principles, because they are so logical. They deal with simple and concrete solutions. They are very much a matter of 'low-tech – high-touch'. Once, after a management team had spent two afternoons learning about lean innovation, the R&D director told us with great satisfaction and a smile on his face that lean could be translated into 'common sense management'. This ultimately became the name of their lean project.

Lean innovation is not academically challenging or difficult to understand. The challenge is to set the right priorities in order to get things done and to develop an entirely new organizational culture around lean innovation. It isn't easy – just ask the organizations going through the process right now. On the other hand, we find that once an organization starts using the lean terms, something they have never seen before happens. And even their customers notice it.

What Lean Innovation Is Not

Like innovation, the term 'lean' is used in many contexts. And it is certainly something people feel very strongly about. People with no experience in lean innovation often have a very strained relationship with the concept. Even among knowledge workers who are acquainted with lean innovation, opinions vary. We would like to give you a better understanding of lean innovation and its purpose by telling you what it is not.

Lean innovation is not:
- A manufacturing method applied to innovation
- A method that kills creativity and idea generation in innovation
- A way to make employees work faster

Lean Innovation Is Not a Manufacturing Method

One misconception that has often hindered the acceptance of lean innovation is the idea that lean is a manufacturing philosophy that does not make sense in an innovation environment. We do not view lean as a manufacturing philosophy. However, there are a number of significant differences between manufacturing and innovation that must be kept in mind when a company introduces lean in an innovation context.

One of the biggest differences is that manufacturing reproduces a known solution, sometimes making several hundred copies an hour. The ECCO shoe factories, for instance, produce several thousand copies of the same shoe, while in an innovation process the end result is unknown when the process starts. The goal is unknown. It is a learning process. This also makes it difficult to know when an innovation process ends, because there is always more you can learn. One of the key competencies in innovation is knowing when a solution is good enough to be introduced to the customers so value creation can start.

In manufacturing, variation is, by definition, non-value-creating – the more exact the object can be reproduced the better. In innovation, we operate with both value-creating and non-value-creating variation. Some variation is valuable as a necessary prerequisite for creating something new. One example of value-creating variation is developing solutions, testing them and then re-doing them. Another is talking to the customer and then adjusting your priorities.

Examples of non-value-creating variation include making collaboration more difficult, creating misunderstandings and unproductive confusion. Some things are consciously subjected to variation, while for other things – like budgets or lead times – we want to establish a degree of predictability. One challenge faced by people who work with product development is recognizing the difference between variation that creates value and variation that just creates waste.

In manufacturing, all the criteria are known in advance. You know what requirements the finished product needs to live up to. At the end of every production line in ECCO's shoe factories, there is a physical example of the perfect shoe which every shoe coming off the line is compared to. If it does not look exactly like that shoe, it cannot be approved. Instead, it is sent back to the relevant production area, which ensures compliance with the standard. In innovation processes, we do not necessarily know all the requirements at the beginning of the process. The criteria are developed continuously as part of the process. For example, say that during the development of a shoe you find out that consumers are willing to pay 25 percent more for a model if a few extra details are added. If these details only increase production costs by 5 percent, the innovation process must be able to handle this change. However, the more variation we can place at the beginning of the innovation process, the better it is.

In innovation, then, the 'object' is what you are working with – ideas, attitudes and knowledge. In some cases, material objects are also involved, such as prototypes or physical models of various types. For example, in shoe design, the end result of the development process is knowledge in the form of drawings, prototypes and tools for manufacturing soles and lasts.

In manufacturing, we deal only with physical objects. We work with tangible start and end products as well as a physical transformation process that is easy to understand. If materials accumulate or the production processes come to a standstill, work-in-progress will immediately start piling up in the production areas. In innovation, most of the processes take place in the minds of the employees, and the knowledge we work with is rarely visible. That is why employee motivation and commitment are more important in lean innovation than in lean manufacturing.

Regardless of where lean is implemented, it has the same philosophical point of departure – that of continuously improving how we work. But lean can never be the same in manufacturing, administration and innovation, because each environment consists of different processes. See Figure 3.2.

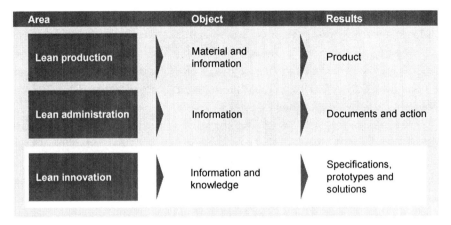

Area	Object	Results
Lean production	Material and information	Product
Lean administration	Information	Documents and action
Lean innovation	Information and knowledge	Specifications, prototypes and solutions

Figure 3.2. Lean in Different Environments

Lean Innovation Does Not Kill Creativity

Doesn't lean affect creativity? This question is rooted in the misconception that the purpose of lean is to cut costs and remove all process activities that cannot be justified in rational terms. For some people this conjures up images from Charlie Chaplin's *Modern Times*, where the workers at the advent of industrialism are lined up in a Taylorist setting along a conveyor belt, doing tedious operations over and over again at an unreasonably fast pace set mechanically by the speed of the conveyor belt.

The question is also rooted in the understanding that creativity requires space for wild ideas, near misses, reflection, experimentation, errors and misunderstandings. Problem-solving is a learning process, and any good learning environment ensures time for trial and error. Focus must also be on progress to ensure that ideas meet 'reality' as quickly as possible, because that is where you learn the most.

There is a need for both structure and freedom in innovation. To heighten awareness of this, we often ask knowledge workers initiating a lean innovation process one key question: "How can lean either destroy or strengthen creativity?" Examples fly through the air: "If we talk to each other more…; if we spend less time on routine tasks, we will have more time for innovation…; if we could spend less time on documentation…; if we were better at keeping our promises…" and in contrast: "If we don't have time to meet over a cup of coffee…; if we are being constantly measured and controlled…;, if we only follow a set of standards…; if we are treated like battery hens…" There are often excellent arguments both for and against lean in the innovation process.

In a way, every comment is relevant, because it is possible to organize our processes so as to strengthen creativity. But we can also inadvertently make life more difficult for ourselves. The point, of course, is to think things through. One challenge is that people are different and everyone works best under different conditions. Many of the people who work with innovation are good at independent thinking and have their own opinions about what is good and what is bad – that is why they work with innovation. But we do not work alone, and innovation is not a one-man show.

Excessive focus on structure, follow-up and documentation is a sure-fire way to destroy creativity. But disorder and confusion can also have a negative impact on creativity. For most people, a reasonable framework and direction for a team's work increases motivation and, thereby, creativity.

Lean Innovation Is Not a way to Make People Work Faster

You could say that a company comprises interaction between four stakeholders: customers, employees, owners and society in general. It should be legitimate to talk about the employees' interests in relation to those of the owners, the customers' interests in relation to those of society etc. Luckily, most companies exist because there is an extremely strong common motivation among these four stakeholders.

When we introduce lean, it is always easy to see the benefits for customers. Customer focus is an important aspect of lean. The customers benefit from both better services and a more efficient mode of production (timely delivery, lower prices, better service etc.). The benefit for the owners is also fairly easy to identify in the form of increased competitiveness, higher returns etc. But what about the employees, what's in it for them? The employees, along with the managers, supply most of the hard work that goes into the lean process. This question often looms large when introducing lean initiatives. The answer depends on what motivates the individual employee. For knowledge workers, curiosity, the opportunity to learn and self-improvement are often high on the agenda. Other important aspects include the chance to be part of a leading and successful organization; improving team skills; reduced waiting times; fewer frustrations and less stress.

The central element of lean, that of eliminating 'waste' and thus freeing up time for what lies at the heart of innovation – i.e. creativity and value-creating development – makes lean innovation interesting to knowledge workers. In fact, the top management is sometimes surprised by the positive effect the increased freedom and responsibility that come with lean has on the level of interest and commitment of their employees.

One of the keys to a positive attitude towards lean is when knowledge workers can see personal, professional and career-related benefits. And this is often
not too difficult once they get started. But it would be wrong to say that there
can be no resistance to lean. It is therefore important to find out what motivates
the employees and to build that into the success criteria for implementing a lean
culture.

The Concept of Waste in Lean Innovation

A simple way to improve efficiency is to eliminate waste. Waste can be found
everywhere once you start looking for it. A good way to increase awareness of
waste is to organize a 'waste workshop' where the employees are encouraged
to think about their own department and processes and identify anything – big
or small – that does not create value. This usually produces a steady flow of
improvement ideas. It is an informal but effective way to identify waste. There
are also more sophisticated approaches that can work quite well. Value stream
mapping and project evaluations, are other ways to identify waste and make
work easier, for your own benefit as well as for your customers.

But before you begin eliminating waste, it is important to ask whether you
are eliminating genuine waste or whether the activity in question is needed to
support the learning process that is inherent in all innovation work. If you do not
remove the right kind of waste, you risk causing a lot of damage. The overview
in Figure 3.3 presents examples of the types of waste you need to be aware of in
innovation processes.

Examples of Waste in Innovation

- Definition of market is too broad and imprecise
- Wrong choices during portfolio process
- Functionalities the customer doesn't need
- Information that isn't translated into relevant insights for
  the solution in question
- Available and relevant knowledge that isn't shared
- Working and testing without learning
- Uncoordinated goals and silo thinking

Figure 3.3. Waste in Innovation

We once heard a project manager in a lean process proudly boasting that they
had reduced the number of prototypes and tests. However, prototypes and testing

are an important part of the innovation process, because they give feedback on solution quality. Of course, in individual cases it may make sense to consider ways to optimize the testing procedures. But viewing prototyping as waste is a definite misunderstanding.

There are two types of waste. The first is product waste, which is delivering something or making unnecessary additions to a product that do not really add value for the customer. The second is process waste, which is when unnecessary work is performed as part of the innovation process.

Product waste is the easiest and most obvious type of waste to eliminate. Going back to the shoe manufacturer ECCO, the company achieved fast results when they held a workshop where the employees in the three departments were given the same assignment. The employees often worked together in the development process, but over time, their processes had become somewhat routine and they did not talk enough with each other about their work. For this exercise, the employees asked all the recipients of their output what they used it for and whether it added value for them. It turned out that many of the reports, drawings and other documents they produced were actually not used by the recipients. This made it easy to eliminate a number of waste-generating processes and documents.

Lean Innovation – Three Parallel Goals

There are three dimensions to achieving efficiency through lean innovation: outer efficiency, inner efficiency and the principle of continuous improvement. In the following, we will explain a little more about lean by taking a closer look at the three dimensions and explaining the thoughts behind each.

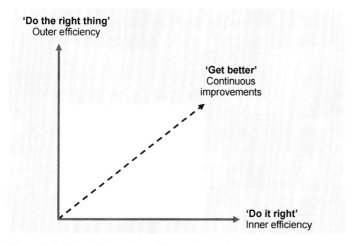

Figure 3.4. Three Dimensions of Lean Innovation

1. 'Do the right thing' – outer efficiency

The point of departure for lean is value, i.e. the value that is created for the recipients at the end of the innovation process. Working with innovation and finding solutions for needs is not something you do for your own sake, but for the benefit of the people who will ultimately use the solution. Many complex problems are solved during an innovation process, as illustrated with wicked problems. However, it can be difficult to imagine making something efficiently for a recipient you have no contact with.

Hopefully, it is clear that you have to take an outside-in approach to innovation. The lazy person's and the smart person's paths to efficiency are the same: to ensure that the recipients value what is produced during the innovation process. Everything else is waste.

As a developer, you have a huge responsibility in the innovation process. Not only does your position early in the value chain give you a lot of influence on the value creation process, you also have control over a variety of expenses throughout the company. The solution you deliver, regardless of whether it is a new process, product or service, will be triggering significant operational costs.

Often, people expect an innovation process to produce specific results right away. In the early phases, however, it is crucial not to get into 'solution mode' too fast. It is important that you understand the need you are trying to fulfill through the innovation process. It can be difficult to evaluate the quality and effort involved in such work from the outside. Therefore, the people involved in the innovation process need to be able to question the quality and efficiency of their own work.

The projects are often not very clearly defined, and the objectives and success criteria are not sufficiently clarified with the person requesting the work. Everyone should feel it is their responsibility to stop any work that is not properly defined.

One potential source of confusion about project objectives is the fact that they continually change. This further underlines the importance of collaborating closely with the users during the innovation process. This can be ensured throughout the development process by testing prototypes in the form of drawings, descriptions, models etc. However, time must be allocated to the development and testing of these prototypes during the innovation process. Some may feel that a development process based on continuous dialog with the recipient places extra pressure on employees because it leaves them with less time to work for themselves. But a process involving close dialog with the recipient is a necessary investment.

2. 'Do it right' – inner efficiency

Inner efficiency is about how we are organized internally around the project we are carrying out for a recipient. This is where value stream mapping becomes a key concept in lean. A value stream is another term for a process and describes the series of activities that help transform a need into a solution, raw materials into a product etc. You can map the entire value stream − from the customers' needs until the customer holds the solution in his or her hand − or you can map parts of it.

In an innovation project, the project plan is the value stream, because this is the process that transforms a need into a solution. Value stream mapping works well because it follows the solution or product that creates value for the customer. Often, value stream mapping will span several different functions and departments. It helps us focus on what the customer is paying for. Value stream mapping can also be used to optimize inner efficiency. If a step in the process does not add value to the product for the customer, it makes sense to look at it with critical eyes.

Value streams are easier to study and analyze in an administration or manufacturing context, because the same process is carried out over and over again. Thus, the ideal in these situations is a uniform and stable process every time, which can be controlled and optimized to perfection. Maintaining a stable process has many advantages in relation to efficiency and, especially, to the quality of the product.

However, in lean innovation, it is not quite that simple. Here, we need to differentiate between transactional and heuristic processes. Transactional processes are predictable processes that are the same every time. Heuristic processes are exploratory and, thus, unpredictable and unique. In our studies of innovative processes, we have found that transactional processes represent a major share of the workload. But they are given little consideration by employees. The opposite is the case with heuristic processes. It is important to understand the difference between these two types of processes because they must be handled differently. Transactional processes are similar to manufacturing processes, and the principles and methods that produce good results in the factory also work for the transactional processes in innovation. The heuristic processes, on the other hand, encourage investigation and learning. They are unpredictable processes that could go on forever. Heuristic processes can be optimized by asking whether the methods used in the process really are the most ideal for generating the knowledge you are looking for.

3. 'Get better' – continuous improvements

The term in Japanese for continuous improvement is *kaizen*. The principle is a rebellion against the 'Big Bang' theory or the idea that if you can just think long enough and hard enough, you can produce the most mind-boggling impact all at once. When you embrace continuous improvements, you believe that making small improvements frequently is better than making major improvements once in a while. A fundamental aspect of continuous improvements is the improvement loop: Plan-Do-Check-Act. The PDCA loop is also called the Deming loop, named after Dr. W. Edwards Deming, who was one of the pioneers of the Total Quality movement in the 1960s and 1970s.

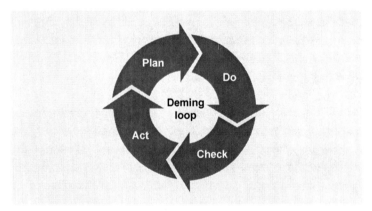

Figure 3.5. Continuous Improvements, PDCA Loop (Deming Loop)

When a company adopts the concept of continuous improvements, it establishes a philosophy and a system for constantly doing things better. And even though it may already be among the best, it does not rest on its laurels – it continues to turn every stone in search of areas where improvements can be made.

Continuous improvements are possible on several levels, and make sense individually, in relation to processes and at corporate level. There are definite advantages for companies with a 'continuous' flow of new product launches compared to companies that produces one breakthrough every eight years:

- They learn faster from 'the real world'.
- They are considered more innovative in the marketplace.
- They cash in on new knowledge at a higher rate.

For knowledge-based organizations, in particular, progression through the PDCA loop should be as fast as possible, because you only learn something once you complete the entire loop. And the more times you complete the loop, for example over a period of a week, the more new knowledge you will acquire.

But wouldn't it be easier to group it together; isn't learning a lot every Friday just as good? Unfortunately, that is not always possible because you might need what you learned on Monday to make your work on Tuesday more insightful, and so on. Consciously working with continuous improvements strengthens a team's ability to collaborate on innovation. It also generates value, which may be lost when working in an 'introverted' and silo-oriented process over extended periods of time.

To be good at continuous improvements, you need to be able to handle feedback. You need to actively seek it out and view it as something helpful rather than a disruption in your work. And in order to integrate continuous improvements in your work processes, feedback should not be viewed as criticism of your work in progress.

Key Principles for Lean Innovation

There are a number of principles that are key to the process of converting knowledge to value. These principles should be part of everything you do, forming a unifying theme. That is why it is not enough to just read the following and agree that it makes sense. That is a good start, of course, but anyone who wants to be a professional developer needs to live according to these principles in everything they do. The principles are important when facing major challenges, but especially when dealing with minor problems. It is often in the little, off-guard situations that you reveal what you really stand for.

Seven key principles for lean innovation:

1. Gemba
2. Front loading
3. Visual management
4. Timeboxing
5. One-piece flow
6. Takt
7. Prototyping

Everyone involved in developing solutions can benefit from these principles. This includes project managers with overall responsibility for solution development. It includes the specialists responsible for building up and maintaining the competencies that should flow into the services the company provides. And, most importantly, it includes the top management, which focuses on both the business-oriented and the value-oriented direction of the company. In other words: The principles apply to all knowledge workers within the company.

The company can only benefit fully from lean if every key player in the company is willing to live by the key lean principles. And that is not as easy as it sounds. It means that they have to think about how they work and how they interact with others.

Luckily it is not necessary to master these principles in the course of a single weekend. In every good lean process, there is time to step back, reflect and try things out as you go along.

1. Gemba

To 'go to gemba' means going to the place where the 'truth is found'. This principle is about understanding what happens in real life by experiencing it for yourself before saying how a problem should be solved.

Taiichi Ohno, who was an executive at Toyota for many years, perfected the process now known as the 'Ohno Circle'. Ohno made it a practice to personally visit any area of production where he was considering making improvements. He would pull out a piece of chalk and draw a circle on the concrete floor. He would then step into the circle and stand there for an hour or more. As he stood there, he would observe everything that took place around him: When new materials were delivered to the production line, how people worked together, what kinds of problems developed and how people reacted to them.

Ohno became wiser in several ways from standing in the circle. Firstly, he obtained a better understanding of the real-life situation, and that knowledge made him a better decision maker. Secondly, he sent a powerful signal to the employees. He showed them that he was interested in what took place and that he was actually willing to spend time understanding the processes.

The gemba principle of understanding what takes place is relevant to many areas of knowledge work. The most obvious is in relation to the users of the solution you are developing or improving. The design firm IDEO has built 'go to gemba' into the innovation process they call 'The Deep Dive'. They do not use the Japanese term *gemba*, but they do the same thing when they send their employees out into the field at the start of a project to observe how customers receive an existing product. Armed with Polaroid cameras, voice recorders, pad and pencil, they try to understand what kinds of problems the customer runs into when he or she orders, pays for and uses a product.

In the book *Blue Ocean Strategy*, the authors Kim and Marbourgne say that in order to create breakthrough concepts it is absolutely necessary to send even the top management out into the field to experience how the customers receive the products.

The gemba principle is especially important for the steadily increasing numbers of service companies and for consulting firms, because these types of businesses create solutions in close collaboration with their customers. But co-creation also takes place in product companies. For example, LEGO is known for involving lead users actively in their development work. They control a highly complex network of 'private' developers located all over the world. This is open innovation, co-creation and gemba in the most extreme.

When it comes to managing innovation projects, gemba also makes very good sense. Does the management have time to visit the projects in the environments where they are being carried out? Does the steering committee demand presentations in a sterile boardroom far from where the project is actually carried out? Or does it take place in the project room where you can see the work in progress? What is more important – the comfort of the management or the success of the project?

When you, as a developer, are charged with designing a product that is optimized for production, you could ask the production manager for a report, but you could also visit the factory floor and talk to the people who work there. And if you, as a project manager, need a specific deliverable from another department, you could, of course, send an e-mail. But you could also walk over there and talk to the person in question, and thus demonstrate that the deliverable is so important that you are willing to spend time trying to understand any challenges affecting the work. One of our close colleagues always says: "As a project manager, your most important tool is your shoes."

Going to gemba on a regular basis is not easy. It takes time, and you will probably have to change how you prioritize your time throughout the day. Do you have the time? How occupied are you with your own personal to-do list? What do you think about colleagues who spend their morning observing customers buying and using your products? Are they wasting their time or generating insights?

Professional knowledge workers should have a burning desire to understand and help the users of the company's solutions.

2. Front loading

All innovation projects start with a very limited understanding of how the future solution will turn out. This is especially true for projects aiming to create something truly novel. This is what makes such projects at once both exciting and frustrating. And oddly enough, the most important decisions are actually made in the early stages of projects, when the knowledge level is at its lowest. Typically, 75 percent of a product's total life cycle cost is defined a quarter of the way through an innovation project.

Front loading aims to increase the knowledge level in the beginning of a project. And it is generally only possible by consuming more resources in the beginning. Of course, it can also be achieved by working smarter. The term 'front loading' actually means to allocate more resources to the project from the outset. Front loading is also postponing decisions until sufficient information is available. Some developers like to call this 'back loading'. But technically it is the same thing: loading up more knowledge in front of a decision.

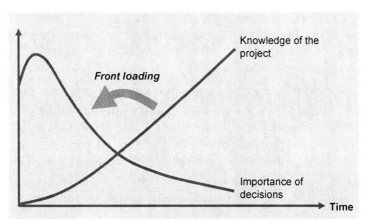

Figure 3.6. Front Loading

There are several ways to achieve front loading. In the 1990s, Toyota became known for developing cars at a fast pace by postponing decision-making. Many other companies work with front loading as well.

A few years ago, the financial institution Nordea Life & Pensions decided to begin developing a new pension product. They chose to allocate more resources level during the conceptual phase of the project in order to systematically explore three different concepts concurrently over an extended period of time. This is actually a very difficult decision to make. It is more costly, and many product specialists and managers are convinced that because of their many years of experience they know full well what the best solution is. But by working with three extreme concepts, Nordea Life & Pensions successfully developed a realistic solution that would have been difficult to achieve through a traditional sequential development process. One of the world's most influential strategists, Gary Hamel, hit the nail on the head when he said: "You can't find new land with an old map."

When IDEO was asked to design a new supermarket shopping cart, they started by brainstorming all the questions that could impact the success of the final solution. Then, the team went into the field – to gemba – to find the answers, i.e. to speak to supermarkets, customers, safety regulators, families with small children and nannies. After their excursion, the team shared what they had learned, thus increasing the level of common knowledge and forming a solid foundation for the subsequent development process. This, too, is front loading.

Front loading is learning faster as individuals but more importantly as a team. It is hard not to agree with this goal. But it isn't always easy to know how, where and how much to front load.

To determine whether you need more knowledge before making a decision, ask yourself the following questions:

- Is impatience a part of our corporate culture or professional background, causing decisions to be made too quickly?
- What is the probability of making a wrong decision? And what are the consequences?
- Does anyone outside the team possess knowledge that can be used in the decision-making process?
- What methods can be used to front load and accelerate knowledge acquisition?

Taking a structured approach to the above questions can help you avoid creating waste when you spend time and resources on increasing the knowledge level at the beginning of a project.

3. Visual Management

They say a picture is worth a thousand words. Perhaps, you could also say that a prototype is worth a thousand pictures, and to take it a step further, that a real-life customer test is worth a thousand prototypes. The essence is the same: Visualization can help you imagine a future situation or solution. Visualization can also help make discussions with others about that future and how to get there more specific.

| Rooms should reflect the work carried out in them | Decorate your workplace | Each room should be different |

Figure 3.7. Pictures Communicate Better Than Words

Visualization is relevant for describing a solution, but also for management or work processes. Visualizing solutions will be covered later under 'prototyping'. Here, we will focus on visualizing management and work processes.

Employing visualization in our work can be as simple as writing a list of decisions and action points on a flip chart in a meeting to confirm that they reflect the discussion among participants. Using a large board or brown paper to keep track of the team's visions and goals is also visualization. Good ideas and decisions can be regularly added to the board using Post-its, making it clear to all team members what the important themes are. They are all posted on the board – including the problem areas. Achieving an efficient visual process requires a willingness to be open about problems and to visually demonstrate responsibility for taking action.

In a project process, visualizing the progress of the plan can be a fantastic way to establish a shared vision, coordination and sense of responsibility among participants.

Goals and project processes can also be visualized using PowerPoint as well as the many graphic tools that popular with communication departments and advertising agencies. Such presentations can be a good idea once in a while, and it often feels good to see your ideas presented in a nice and professional way. But 'professional' communication has its drawbacks as well. It is costly, takes longer and is harder to change, unless you are a PowerPoint or Illustrator specialist. Furthermore, such presentations may end up only documenting something that has already happened. They can be outdated before they are even finished.

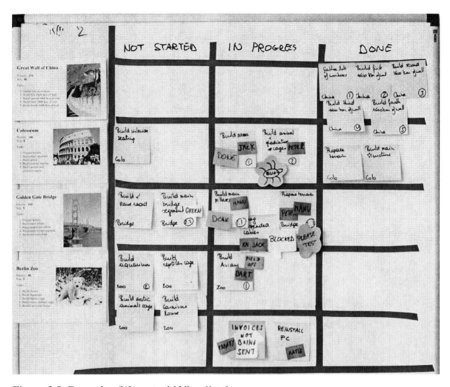

Figure 3.8. Example of 'Low-tech' Visualization

We recommend a low-tech approach to visualization. You can actually do quite a lot with not much more than markers, Post-its and brown paper. A plan made using Post-its on a calendar board encourages more participation and debate than a fancy PowerPoint presentation does. Low-tech tools are better at promoting two-way communication. And two-way communication is a critical aspect of knowledge work.

Sometimes we hear someone say that using Post-its and brown paper in a meeting seems weak and childish. In fact, it is quite a demanding process, because problems are discussed openly and because decisions and responsibilities are delegated in front of everyone. Visual management supports the innovation process in both form and focus.

4. Timeboxing

'Timeboxing' is when you operate with a fixed lead time so the end time for a deliverable is set in stone.

At the start of an innovation project, not all the specifications for the solution are available. This information is systematically gathered during the project process. Under these conditions, and especially if it has been difficult to clearly define the project objectives, it may not be easy to say when the solution is good enough. All innovation and knowledge work is learning, and because learning is a never-ending process, it is necessary to set a fixed deadline for when the work must stop.

To support the predictability and speed that should characterize the solutions, it is necessary to meet specific deadlines for delivery. That goes for the company and the project as a whole, but also for sub-solutions, deliverables and milestones within the project process.

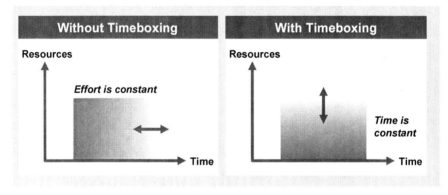

Figure 3.9. Timeboxing

Everyone has experienced situations when delivery has been postponed by others – or even worse, by yourself – because the product could still be tweaked just a little more. That is a fine ambition; however, that kind of behavior is also poison for any innovation system because it triggers an unfortunate domino effect throughout the entire project or organization

If there is a risk that a deadline cannot be met, the first response must be to add more resources. Then you need to assess whether any product functionalities not specifically requested by the customer can be removed. A timebox can also be a useful frame for managing work. Say, for instance, that you are working on a report or a presentation; deciding that it has to be delivered within three hours can help you plan your work better. It can also be quite a liberating thought: 'I'll do my best in three hours, and then take it from there.' It is vital that we keep our promises, both individually and collectively, because others depend on it and because we have made a personal, public and visual promise to do so.

5. One-piece flow

Imagine a warm and sunny summer day. You are standing on your patio getting ready to start working in the garden. Your neighbor has complained about your hedges, your lawn is looking scruffy and the flower bed is overrun by weeds. You are enjoying the last of your coffee while contemplating the best way to proceed.

It wouldn't make much sense to trim one-third of the hedge, cut half the lawn and then weed one corner of the flower bed. That would also be an inefficient way to work. You would have to take all your gardening tools out of the garage and put them back again several times. You would progress along the experience curve just to be forced to start over for each activity. Consequently, it would take longer for the work to create value. It would be better to be able to show your wife or husband a completely trimmed hedge at 5 pm rather than three half-finished gardening jobs.

When a company works with knowledge, it is not uncommon to feel that your work is fragmented and to be involved in five or six different initiatives in the course of a day. This can leave you feeling like you are not really getting anything done.

This same challenge also exists at corporate level. How many important priorities are there at once? The more concurrent innovation projects, the less focus there is on each one. And, of course, both people and companies need to be able to work on several priorities at once. But companies and developers have a natural tendency to keep too many balls up in the air.

Increasing focus on one-piece flow – or doing one thing at a time – has a number of advantages for both individuals and companies.

- It increases concentration and immersion, thus resulting in a higher-quality solution.
- Less time passes before the knowledge that is generated can be used by others and thereby create value.
- It more frequently produces a feeling of completing something, which results in greater satisfaction.
- Less time is wasted on switching between tasks, thus lowering costs and reducing irritation.

For instance, when you attend a meeting, do you help close one topic before a new one is opened? When planning work, be it your own or that of others, do you make sure to allocate the time and resources needed to do the job properly? What produces the most respect and recognition within the company – talking a lot and keeping a hundred balls in the air or finishing one task properly before starting the next?

6. Takt

Try placing your index finger on your opposite wrist and counting your pulse beats. If you have time to read this book, you are probably relatively relaxed. You will most likely have a pulse of between 50 and 70 beats per minute, and the beats will likely have a very regular rhythm or 'takt'. It would be unhealthy for the body if the heart produced three beats in one second followed by five seconds with no beats, and so forth. Knowing full well that we are moving outside our particular area of expertise, it does make good sense for the heart to beat regularly. A regular heart rhythm is important because other parts of the body need to receive a steady flow of oxygen and nutrients.

Like the body, a company can also be seen as a living organism. Maintaining a regular and predictable rhythm, such as holding a departmental meeting every Friday between 9 and 10 am, means that other parts of the organism (the company) know when decisions will be made and discussions will take place. A company's operation has a takt, and development and innovation should also have a takt. The guiding takt for innovation is the pipeline or the launch plan for new products and services. You could call this the heartbeat of innovation. This rhythm should be regular so the organism does not become overheated or feverish.

Takt is also relevant within the individual innovation project. If the project participants do not know when their deliverables need to be ready and if these deliverables are not evenly distributed over time, the project team can become stressed and frustrated. A good and even takt for management, innovation output, deliverables and project milestones has many advantages:

- Greater predictability in the innovation process
- Production is more even, thus avoiding unnecessary strain on the system
- More systematic opportunities to receive feedback – supporting continuous improvements
- More progress is made

Won't an even takt make the work boring? Many creative and dynamic people love the energy that is generated as the date for a customer presentation, trade fair or fashion show draws near.

Imagine an ad agency having to present a branding concept to an important customer. Two weeks before the presentation is due, the team is rushing around like crazy. The agency director personally contributes good ideas for the project. The project team puts in long hours to realize the best ideas. Any problems that occur need to be solved quickly – also the seemingly insignificant ones. The plotter breaks down, and after tough negotiations with printers out of town, their project is moved to the front of the printer's production pipeline. Yes, way to go! A project participant grabs a cab and drives out to the printers. The driver gets an extra tip if he can speed it up. After the material is printed, everything is rushed back to the office where all the material is gathered together. They run through the material and the agenda for the presentation. Partners, the project manager and the branding specialist rush out to the customer. They get there three minutes before their presentation is due. The presentation is lively and energetic, everyone is pleased with the result and the ad agency lands the job.

Everyone feels great as they gather in the bar that evening for a toast. Surviving a crisis together is energizing and produces a sense of having created value. Unfortunately, this feeling also arises when you solve a self-made crisis. How much customer value is there in spending three hours negotiating with the printers and picking up the material in a cab? That time could have been spent improving the content of the customer's solution. What you should be asking is: How do we create energy that also creates more customer value?

A distinct takt creates energy throughout the course of the project, not just at the last minute. It also sends a clear signal to other parts of the company, or to external stakeholders, about what they can expect and when they can expect it.

7. Prototyping

"Lower the bar for prototyping to increase the rate of learning" – IDEO

Learning and innovation are most successful when the Plan-Do-Check-Act loop functions properly. This means that you are good at continuously improving yourself. In the learning loop, prototyping is placed centrally under the 'check' step. Prototyping is a way of testing assumptions in order to subsequently improve your concept. Prototyping is used in all types of innovation, and is becoming ever more popular. In the 1980s, 30 percent of all organizations used prototypes, in the 1990s, this figure had grown to 60 percent. Examples of prototypes include:

- Functional solutions or partial solutions
- Computer simulations
- Models
- Images/graphics

- Product sheets
- Product ads

Prototypes help you imagine that future which is always unknown in innovation. Prototyping is about visualizing the solution so you can talk about it internally, but also, and even more importantly, so you can discuss it with the user. Prototyping forces you to step outside your own discipline to transform specifications, programming or calculations into something the user can comprehend. It is speaking the language of the user, and is a very useful way to achieve a successful solution.

Isn't making a lot of prototypes waste? Making a lot of strange prototypes that will never reach the shop shelves may seem like waste, but if building prototypes provides you with new knowledge that can be used to improve your concept, then you have actually created value. Here, of course, it is important to remember that cost must be considered in relation to benefit. However, one thing is certain: Prototyping without learning is waste. Prototyping should therefore be a part of the innovation process at both the early and later stages.

Prototypes can be seen as integration points throughout the process, bringing together all the latest insights to form a solution that can be communicated to the user. A prototype must never be the final documentation for the entire process primarily for attracting praise. A prototype is not an advertising gimmick intended to show off how good you are. A prototype should be made because you are trying to find out what needs improving. Prototyping is an integral part of an open, inquisitive and fun innovation process.

It should never feel tiresome to receive a lot of feedback that means you have to change your concept. You should therefore also expect to spend time gathering and working with the newly acquired knowledge after testing a prototype. As a rule, twice as much time should be spent making changes as is spent building the prototype and planning the test.

Producing a lot of prototypes makes sense because every prototype generates learning. Consequently working with low-tech prototypes, yes, even if they are made from cardboard and paper, is often an advantage. It is less expensive, it is fast and it is more legitimate to propose changes when it does not look like a million bucks. This is especially the case when it is for use in-house. However, a prototype must never be so simple or commonplace that this fact becomes the focal point of the potential user's feedback. With regard to prototyping as a principle, or as a state of mind, it may be worthwhile to consider two things:

1. How strong is my customer focus? Am I good at creating images that give a customer or user an idea of what is being created? How well do I speak the user's language?

2. How oriented am I towards improvements? Am I willing to show half-finished work as a solution or present images in order to obtain new knowledge? Does feedback bother me, and would I rather perfect my work before subjecting it to the criticism of others?

Literature:

Chan, Kim W. & Renée Mauborgne: *Blue Ocean Strategy*. Harvard Business School Press, 2005.

Deming, Dr. W. Edwards: *Some Theory of Sampling*. Wiley & Sons, New York, 1950.

Hardgrave, Bill C. & Rick L. Wilson: "An Investigation of Guidelines for Selecting a Prototyping Strategy". *Journal of Systems Management*, 1994.

Kelley, Tom: The Art of Innovation: Lessons in Creativity from IDEO, America's Leading Design Firm. Profile Books, 2001.

Poppendieck, Mary & Tom: *Implementing Lean Software Development*, Addison-Wesley Signature Series, 2003.

Reinertsen, Donald G.: Managing the Design Factory: A Product Developer's Toolkit. The Free Press, 1997.

Reinertsen, Donald G.: "How Product Development Sparked a Revolution". *Industrial Engineer*, June 2005.

Ward, Allen C.: *The Lean Development Skills Book*. Ward Synthesis, Inc. 2002.

Ward, Allen C.: *Lean Product and Process Development*. Lean Enterprise Institute, Cambridge 2007.

Part III
Achieving Success with Lean Innovation

Chapter 4
Releasing the Potential for Innovation

Most companies have a huge untapped potential for increasing innovation value through their existing systems, collective experience and dedicated employees. The possibilities for creating extra value early in the value chain, where the solutions are developed are practically endless. Success is really only limited by the imagination.

When it comes to the existing objectives and tasks, development organizations perform very well, for the most part. But there may be significant opportunities for the entire company to raise its ambitions and transform the entire innovation system into a strategic capability. In our experience, knowledge workers in development departments are technically very good at what they do. But we also find that they rarely take a step back and ask themselves how they could do things even better. There is significant potential for improving how development work is carried out.

Think about the potential for improvement in your own innovation processes. Is it possible to increase the level of ambition and the 'buy-in' to your visions? Where could the processes generate more customer value? And can any waste be eliminated? Try making a mental list of the biggest improvement opportunities in your company. Most likely, you can quickly identify dozens of areas that could be improved, thereby confirming that the potential is there. But that is the easy part of the exercise. Normally, it isn't too difficult to point out what needs improving. The hard part is doing something about it. Management thinker David Meister formulated a similar point in his book *Strategy and the Fat Smoker*: It is easy to tell a fat smoker what to do to get healthier. Get more exercise, eat less and quit smoking. But actually making that happen can be quite difficult.

Companies do all kinds of things to create a healthier innovation system: they improve their development processes; the management sharpens its leadership skills; and the knowledge workers enhance their specialist competencies. The challenge they are often left with, however, is how to make it all work together. All too often, we see employees who possess the individual skills needed and who are very knowledgeable, but who do a poor job brining it all together to make it move in a common direction. There is simply too much

C. Sehested, H. Sonnenberg, *Lean Innovation*, DOI 10.1007/978-3-642-15895-7_5,

focus on specialist competencies and individual targets compared to common objectives and the ability to integrate.

A Common Goal for the Company's Innovation

To achieve maximum benefit from innovation work, you need a shared vision that every stakeholder in the innovation system can support. This vision should be a genuine ambition for the employees and should take as its point of departure the fundamental focal point of all innovation: the customer and the value you can create for the customer. The dream everyone should be striving for is the dream of doing something for a group of users that no one has done before. Some are successful. For example, Saxo Bank has successfully developed a unique online trading platform that makes it possible for ordinary people to trade securities. And the pharmaceutical company Novo Nordisk has invented the successful NovoPen, which has made life easier for millions of people with diabetes.

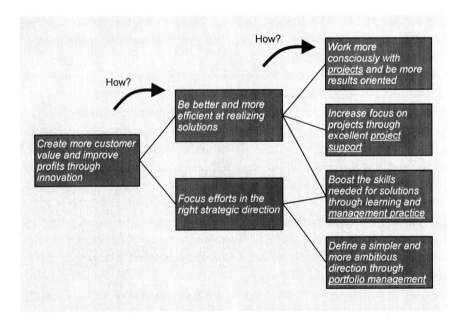

Figure 4.1. Break Down of Innovation Effect

But in order to achieve success without getting lost in a vast, gray sea of conflicting goals, everyone in the organization needs to focus on where value is created. They need to focus on the core process of innovation, which starts with a customer need and progresses through a conscious choice of direction in the innovation process to ultimately create value. The management, project support and any other support functions need to establish the best possible framework for the innovation process. To improve the results of the innovation process, it may be helpful to take a closer look at the concept of 'effect'. The flow of improvements becomes more insightful, specific and coordinated when the most important underlying objectives are well-defined.

The innovation system can be viewed as four areas, each with their own set of individual sub-targets that support the overall vision. The four areas have their own unique roles and responsibilities in the overall system. When all four areas begin developing both their individual and their cross-functional competencies at the same time, the effect on the implementation of an improvement philosophy like lean is amplified.

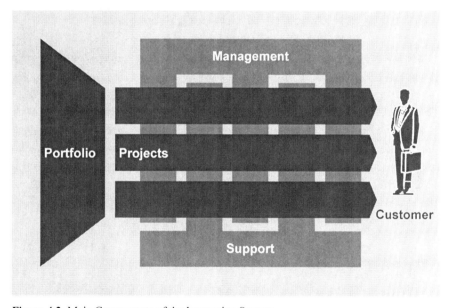

Figure 4.2. Main Components of the Innovation System

There is huge potential for developing these areas on an individual basis, thus generating specific improvements and increasing the efficiency of the knowledge work. But there is much more potential in optimizing how the individual areas interact. For instance, we have seen support functions spend time and resources optimizing internal documentation processes that were not part of the 'critical path' of the projects.[1] As a result, the employees became disappointed over time because they had optimized something that was not really visible in the overall results of the organization. If the support functions had started by initiating a dialog with the people involved in the projects about how they could contribute to their performance, they would probably have chosen to optimize other processes. It is bad enough that the employees became disappointed, but what may be even worse is the fact that the limited management resources that are available for implementing improvements were wasted on something with no immediate and visible customer value.

The effect of the improvements will not really reach the customers until every area in the innovation process shares the same objective and speaks the same language when it comes to improvements.

Lean in the Main Parts of the Innovation System

Figure 4.2 shows the innovation system most commonly found in a competitive organization. However, a similar structure can also be found, either implicitly or explicitly, in other organizations where people work together to create something new. The ideas come from somewhere, they are executed through some form of project-like process, and during the realization process, the ideas need management, resources and other support along the way. It does not really matter exactly how the innovation system is organized, as long as everyone contributing to the innovation has a common language they can use when talking about it. Here, we would like to call attention to four areas where optimization can be beneficial: management, the portfolio, projects and project support.

Management

By management, we mean everyone from the executive management to function-level managers. Management covers the processes that extend beyond the projects and the line organization. The management processes define the direction for the organization and prioritize resources. Through its work, the management should establish the optimum framework in the organization and ensure that the dynamics between projects and the line organization are as fruitful as possible. Every effort should be made by the management to create the best environment for innovation within the organization in both the short and

---

[1] In project management, the 'critical path' is the sequence of activities that impact on the project's lead time. Any delay in one activity in that sequence will extend the project's lead time.

long term. It is management's job to develop the organization. Identifying and developing the competencies needed to achieve quality and focus in the innovation process is the responsibility of the management, and especially the discipline leaders.

The portfolio

Portfolio management translates the company's visions into action through projects. The portfolio strategy involves deciding which combination of innovation projects will best support the company's own strategy and the marketing strategies. Depending on whether the main focus is radical new solutions, technology development or product maintenance, the innovation resources are brought into play in various ways. Portfolio management establishes healthy conditions for the individual projects while ensuring balance in the portfolio as a whole. Portfolio management is the key to ensuring uniform consumption of the company's resources and to utilizing them in a reasonable manner through capacity management and staffing.

Projects

There can be no doubt that projects attract a lot of attention. Most, if not all, companies take a project-oriented approach to innovation. This is because project work is well-suited to the flexibility required by the assignments. The innovation process is integrated and coordinated within projects, and that is also where most of the innovation work takes place. How broadly the projects are defined tends to vary. Some companies operate with very narrowly defined projects, with the work in the project teams consisting almost entirely of coordination. Other companies' projects are broader, with a large share of the work taking place in project teams and with team members collaborating with people from all over the organization. Regardless of their scope, however, all projects are responsible for delivering a solution to a need and there is always a customer 'waiting' at the end of the project process.

Project Support

Most projects maintain some sort of interaction with the rest of the organization, including the line organization. The line organization's job is to support the projects. Often, the line organization performs specific tasks at the request of the projects, acting as a kind of subsupplier. For example, a patent department might be asked to examine the patentability of inventions or discoveries made during the course of the projects. The responsibilities vary greatly from large-scale tasks during actual development work to purely operational tasks, such as experiments and testing with regard to standards, drawing up bills of materials in ERP systems, recruitment and financial management.

The support organization generally takes a more long-term perspective on things and has greater opportunity to benefit from learning across projects. The processes in the support organization are more likely to resemble the processes in manufacturing rather than project processes. Because the support organization provides support to several projects at once, one of its biggest challenges is being able to handle the unpredictable and changing needs of projects.

In the next chapter, we will examine how to bring lean innovation into play in order to achieve the greatest possible effect for the company as a whole. We will also look at how this has been done through examples and models that can act as inspiration in your improvement process.

Literature:

Maister, David H.: Strategy and the Fat Smoker, Doing What's Obvious But Not Easy. The Spangle Press, 2008.

Chapter 5
Active and Visible Management

With an inspiring and motivational style, management can instill a sense of ownership and energy in the knowledge work. And by maintaining focus on visions, ambitions and follow-up, the management can help translate this energy into results for the benefit of the company. This makes management the single most important factor when it comes to creating innovation processes that realize the strategic objectives through speed and predictability. The difference in the effect produced by an average leader and a great leader is enormous. The significant results by such icons as Jack Welch, Steve Jobs and Richard Branson can be directly tied to great leadership.

The leader's potential to inspire employees is key, when it comes to both running the business processes and establishing lean as an innovation culture. The manager's behavior and ownership is the deciding factor for how well lean will work in the organization. The manager is also responsible for making lean innovation work optimally. And the lean principles can help the manager improve his or her leadership skills. Not only can lean can be a good support in the daily management tasks in the knowledge-based organization, it can also promote the process of continuous improvement in the value-creating processes.

Lean in management is all about incorporating the principles of lean into your leadership style. Managers can use lean in four areas to help strengthen their leadership skills:

- Focus on customer-oriented processes
- Regular routines for continuous improvements
- More systematic management in coordination with colleagues
- A more visible and active management style

In this chapter, we will take a closer look at these areas and provide real-life examples of how lean has influenced the way some leaders think and act.

C. Sehested, H. Sonnenberg, *Lean Innovation,* DOI 10.1007/978-3-642-15895-7_6,
© Springer-Verlag Berlin Heidelberg 2011

Lean Is a Leadership Philosophy

Most managers expect lean to be about introducing new methods for solving the problems that exist in their organization. True, it is possible to implement some parts of the lean toolbox and achieve an immediate effect. But if you want to make significant improvements in your organization, it will quickly become clear that much of your dissatisfaction with the organization is, at least partly, the result of your attitude towards leadership and how you practice it. You will quickly find a number of conditions that point back to the manager and that require the manager to change his or her mindset and behavior.

Lean is about how you view the organization and how you interpret your own role within the organization. It is about what you prioritize and where you want to focus your energy. It is about where you choose to place yourself, physically, and what you choose to work with. In short, lean is a leadership philosophy.

Focus on Customer-Oriented Processes

When introducing lean, managers need to think much more in terms of processes, especially the processes that create value for the customer. Useful, stable processes are the key to speed and predictability in the innovation process. We have met many managers who have, over time, lost touch with what is actually takes place in the processes that are so vital for the company.

Instead, the managers have become absorbed in tasks of a more specialist or administrative nature, serving a kind of specialist backbone function in which they follow up on budgets, work with strategy, recruit employees, prioritize initiatives, plan staffing etc. We have a good example of this from a company that started the implementation of a lean innovation program by bringing together the top management to talk about what lean would mean for them. When the discussion came around to customer focus and customer-orientated processes, the CEO asked his department managers to tell him about any improvement initiatives they might recommend. A silence spread across the room, and the managers all stared at each other.

The CEO then called a new meeting with the next level of managers. He talked about lean and asked the same question as at the previous meeting. The reaction was the same – complete silence. The issue was postponed once more, and it was decided that during the following week, the members of the management team would run a parallel process in each middle management department involving both employees and top management.

Each department held a meeting. And the employees were very surprised and honored to be joined by members of the top management. They talked about their work in the development projects. The meeting was very energetic and in the course of an hour, they had produced about 100 specific ideas for simple ways to improve processes.

Only a strong CEO could display this kind of ownership. It took courage for the management to grab the bull by the horns, go directly to the employees on the front line and expose the fact that they did not have control over what was happening in their own processes. It was an eye-opener for the entire organization and it served as a powerful signal to everyone that the tides were changing.

Some might expect their organization to have more insight into its processes than was the case with the company described above. But it is worth considering whether the management could actually do more. Does the management know enough about the processes that span the company's departments from beginning to end, or are they only aware of what happens in their own areas? What specific challenges do the front-line employees experience, and is anyone doing anything about them?

The Upside-Down Organizational Chart

Management's view of its role in a lean organization differs from what is standard in other organizations. The upside-down organizational chart reflects this new way of thinking.

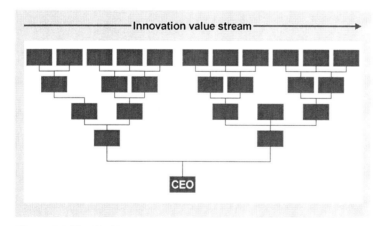

Figure 5.1. The Upside-Down Organizational Chart

The above figure reminds employees and managers of the company's reason for being, i.e. to create value for the customers. It reminds us that it is the responsibility of the management, staff and support functions to support the processes that create customer value. This is a central message in lean, and through lean, the management and the rest of the organization are reminded that it is their job to support and develop the core processes that involve the work of so many employees and that have – either directly or indirectly – a customer at the receiving end.

Ramboll Oil & Gas, Norway, is a good example of the kinds of changes lean can bring. The CEO told us about a realization he had come to while presenting his organization to a customer at a sales meeting. His organizational chart was three pages long. The first page showed the top management with the staff functions, the second page showed the department managers, line managers and support staff, and the third page showed the staff in the project department.

When he reached the third page in the organizational chart, he realized how wrong the presentation was: The first two pages showed the management, support and staff organization comprising approx. 20 employees, while the final page showed the approx.100 people who actually worked for the customer and handled the majority of the contact with the customer's organization throughout the project period.

There was something wrong with the values that this presentation signaled, not only towards the customer, but also towards the management and the employees within the organization. The CEO also noticed that many of the employees in the project department talked about their work as though it took place in the machine room. So they changed the organizational chart to make the large project department more visible on page one. The importance of the organizational chart must never be underestimated as a tool for communicating the management's focus and the employees' understanding of what kind of work is considered important and attractive. The upside-down organizational chart is more than just a diagram on a piece of paper. It also symbolizes the organization's attitude towards and respect for customer-oriented work.

Task Management is a Management Task

The increasing need to focus on processes can be a challenge for many managers, especially in knowledge-based organizations. They are understandably very preoccupied with their professional competencies, and often they have been made managers because they are very good within their area of specialization

– and not necessarily because they are good at driving an efficient organization. They lack the tools and experience from working with processes.

We would like to introduce a method of assessing where your management focus currently stands and where it should be aimed in future. In the following figure, the management task is broken down into four dimensions: management of disciplines, customers, employees and tasks. For most managers, it will be relevant to increase focus on task management, which is what holds the knowledge workers' contributions together. It will also be relevant to minimize focus on managing discipline content.

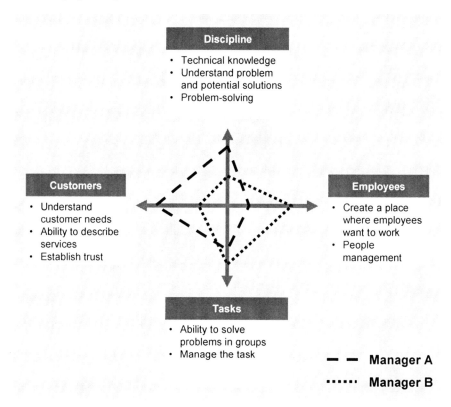

Figure 5.2. The Four Dimensions of the Management Task

1. Discipline management is management of the specialist knowledge and competencies that give the knowledge-based organization its legitimacy. Without a specialist competency that can be used to solve tasks, you could say there would be nothing to do business with. Most managers are aware of this fact and spend a good deal of time and resources enhancing

specialist competencies. In most knowledge-based organizations, this area consumes most of the development resources, often representing 80-90 percent of the investments.

2. The second element is management of customer relations. A company needs to have a good understanding of the customer's point of view, because without that, the company cannot exist. And there would be no demand for the knowledge and services the organization has to offer. Handling customer relations is an important management task. You have to be able to maintain a dialog with customers as well as define their needs. It is crucial that you understand what is to be made and how it is to be delivered.

3. The third element is people management. If this area is not functioning properly, there may soon be only one employee left in the organization – the manager. The management is responsible for ensuring the well-being of their employees, creating motivation, recruiting right talents etc. The value generated by knowledge workers can vary greatly, depending on how motivated, liked and appreciated they feel.

4. The fourth element is task management, which focuses on how we carry out jobs for customers. This includes everything that addresses the challenge finding the best possible way to bring the employees' competencies into play in relation to each other. Task management involves working with processes and methods. And because the dominant working method in knowledge-based organizations is project work, it will, in many cases, also focus on how projects are organized and managed. Task management is just as important as the other management tasks. However, highly discipline-oriented organizations tend to neglect this area because both management and employees are very individualistic and focused on own specialist competencies.

This model can be used to assess where your focus is aimed and can aid discussions about whether that aim is optimal in relation to what the organization as a whole wants to achieve. As mentioned, most companies will need more focus on task management to achieve an efficient organization. It is also worth noting that task management can impact customer and employee satisfaction as well. When projects are well-managed, the customers receive their deliverables on time and the employees are efficient and satisfied.

Management Should Develop the Processes

A lot of managers in specialized, discipline-oriented organizations are uncertain about how to begin focusing on task management. One way to shift away from being a specialist and to become more process-oriented is to think more in terms of 'how' rather than 'what'. When you think in terms of 'how', you automatically focus more on processes and take yourself out of the role of being the expert with all the answers.

This mental transformation is particularly difficult for many managers in knowledge-based organizations because they are so caught up in their specializations. As one employee put it: "It doesn't matter how hard we try to coordinate our work at the Tuesday meetings. As soon as we start discussing a product, everyone starts talking about the technical aspects."

We rarely see managers in knowledge-based organizations with management as their only competency. This is an extra challenge for discipline leaders, and they have to be willing to give up some of their specialization in order to be more active as managers of tasks or processes. In our discussions with managers on this issue, we have found five common causes for this.

Figure 5.3. Discipline Leaders' Excuses for Focusing on Their Specialization

"I'm the best in my field." Many managers in knowledge-based organizations are recruited or promoted because they are the best in their field. Their interest in that field and their identities as specialists are very powerful. So powerful, in fact, that even though they now hold a managerial position, they want to continue to be the best in their field. They forget, however, that their primary focus should now be on helping their employees succeed. Managers – especially in knowledge-based organizations – can find it difficult to let go of their discipline.

In some cases, it may be a good idea to move them out of their own field of expertise for a period of time. This can give managers the opportunity to concentrate more on developing their competencies within task management and increase their focus on the interaction among the employees while executing their tasks. This lets managers tap into their valuable experience as leaders of an organization without being impeded by their own specialist knowledge.

"They don't want me to interfere." Knowledge environments have a tradition, which originates in the academic world, for having the freedom to choose their own working method. The employees are highly educated and intelligent. And since they are capable of solving difficult problems, they should also be able to plan their own work. In some areas, the work process is actually part of the discipline. Some might consider it a bit degrading to talk about processes: "The level is simply too low". Even though small process details can have a huge impact on cooperation and value creation, technical discussions are considered more worthy or intellectual – and more fun. In this context, it is understandable that managers are concerned about their employees reaction to interference in how they work.

"It isn't something I'm good at." Another challenge of a more practical nature is the fact that neither employees nor managers have very much training in working with processes and facilitating process work. Many managers simply lack the necessary competencies and experience.

"There will always be a need for specialists." Another reason managers give for not wanting to shift their focus is that specialization is a kind of job security. The strong focus on specialization can feel like a guarantee that you can still return to an earlier point in your career. It is something the manager knows well. Management is a different discipline that has to be learned, and there is no guarantee that he or she will succeed.

"I'm too busy." Focusing on processes takes time. Many managers feel that they do not have the time or the resources it takes to really begin discussing 'how' the work should be done. There are many processes and sub-processes that need to be addressed, and this can make the task seem impossible. The work needs to be prioritized in relation to other tasks, which is probably the most difficult part.

Many aspects need to be considered if you want to change your approach to management. It takes a great deal of energy to do this on your own. As a consequence, we find that organizations working with lean as a group project actually benefit from having several managers learn something new at the same time. It brings the managers closer together, because introducing a lean culture can be a radical change. This, in turn, encourages closer collaboration and knowledge sharing at management level.

Management Must be Open to Change

How the managers understand the tasks they are expected to perform and the perspective they take in going about those tasks, both, play a significant role in how much an organization can change.

A CEO at a large company once introduced us to the concept of the 'Tarzan swing'. When Tarzan flies through the air on a vine in the jungle, the swing is wider at the bottom than at the top. The CEO used the concept as a warning that what you decide at the top level of the organization will have a significant impact on the lives of many people at lower levels in the organization. For instance, a decision to enter a new market somewhere in the world will start a machinery that will occupy lots of people for many years to come. Some may even have to move abroad with their families. When the top management makes a decision on Friday morning, they need to respect the fact that it can have dramatic consequences for other people.

You could even say that lean is a kind of upside-down Tarzan swing. It may actually be the management that needs to change the most in the process of introducing lean. Is management willing and prepared for that? Does the management have the right structures in place, personally and interpersonally, to embark on this journey of transformation? Each member of the management team needs to have a personal interest in self improvement, otherwise you will quickly discover there is a limit to how far you can come with lean.

From an industrial company, we have a perfect example of how a manager can literally stand in the way of lean. The company was frustrated that their development projects were never finished on time and their employees experienced periods with heavy workloads and stress several times a year. They hoped lean could help change the current situation, increasing both delivery certainty of projects and employee satisfaction at the same time.

A diagnosis of the problem quickly revealed that a key member of the management team, who was highly recognized for his competencies, was a major part of the problem. He, too, wished something could be done about it, and was eager to see results. The top management approached him very carefully as they were concerned about how he would react if they went against his wishes.

Put very simply, it was as though the entire organization of about 50 people worked as his assistants. Every important decision had to pass his desk. The manager was a perfectionist and any decision could be changed – regardless of when it was made. The manager was so overloaded by all the decisions he had to make that he did not have time to reflect on his own role in the problem. When all was said and done, he wasn't all that unhappy with the situation, either, because it appealed to his ego and gave him an energy boost. One of the employees joked that they should hire a baker to do the manager's job. By this he meant a manager who was not burdened by being a specialist in a specific discipline.

Several meetings were held with the manager to try to get him to recognize his own share in the problems experienced by the department. Because it was hard to find time for these meetings, they ended up being spread out over nearly a year, and during that time, very little progress was made to improve the organization. In the end, the meetings did not have the desired effect, because the manager refused to change his behavior. Something more was needed to achieve a breakthrough. Finally, an 'operations manager' was appointed to work parallel with the manager. He was given responsibility for scoping assignments, and slowly things began to change.

The manager in question was placed so high up the hierarchy that the problem could actually be solved by hiring someone as support position instead of getting the manager to change his ways. Many management areas are so small that the manager serves a strong specialist backbone function as well as acting as a personnel manager. In this type of organization, the manager needs to accommodate and differentiate between the different roles.

Working Systematically with Improvements

Implementing lean means that managers will have to work more systematically to develop and maintain the organization.

The following figures show the three classic management tasks plus a fourth that has been added as a consequence of lean. The classic management tasks can be summed up by the following three questions: Why are we here; Where are we going; and How good are we? With lean, we can add a fourth question: How can we get better?

1 Why are we here?

2 Where are we going?

3 How good are we?

4 How can we get better?

Figure 5.4. The Classic Management Questions

We will start by explaining the four questions, and then return to why we have chosen to highlight them when talking about lean.

The first question seeks to explain why we are all here. For many, it will be the same as communicating the objective of the organization. Why should the employee use his or her resources to work for this particular organization and not for a competing company? It is important that the manager returns to this question and answers it on a regular basis.

The second question seeks to explain where we are going. It is the goal of the organization, its success criteria and level of ambition. The answer may be performance targets, but it may also be process targets. For example: What do we need to deliver by the end of the year, and how efficiently do we need to deliver it?

The third question actually expresses management's right and obligation to assess whether the satisfactory results have been achieved. Are our achievements as an organization good enough? Management are responsible for following up on the goals and reacting accordingly – either by changing how something is done or by using rewards and recognition.

The first three questions are what you might call the three classic management tasks. In a lean culture, there is a fourth management task summed up by the question: 'How can we get better?' The fourth management task is not the most dominant task, but every manager should ask him or herself: How can I do achieve this? When can I find the time in my busy schedule, and how will I get it done?

This may sound simple, but many organizations experience uncertainty about these things. We believe there is an efficiency benefit to be gained from taking a consistent approach to these questions.

They are also useful tools for management in a lean culture. If you can answer the first three questions, it is easier to answer the fourth question: "How can we get better?"

A good example of the consequences of not setting targets comes from a chemical company. The executive management was dissatisfied with the results produced by the development. They arranged a meeting with the head of the department to discuss a preliminary study they hoped could shed light on the problems. At the first meeting, after the management talked about the problems, the head of department asked them to explain more clearly what they expected from the department. The room became very quiet. The top management had not defined their expectations for performance. The department was operating on the basis of a declaration of intent. This was reflected in the organization, which did not know what it was supposed to deliver and when something was good enough. Many development departments might recognize similar situations.

One important mechanism in a lean culture is getting the employees involved in discussing the organization's objective, targets and performance so they know what goals to aim for. Equally important is the discussion about the changes – big or small – that are necessary to improve the organization's performance. That is why it makes sense to stick to the four questions even though they may seem trivial. They can form a point of departure for significantly improving efficiency in many knowledge-based organizations.

Management and Continuous Improvements

Supporting continuous improvements is a key element of lean. A central aspect of a lean culture is that every employee makes a conscious effort to identify improvement opportunities and help find solutions that can work in practice. It is the responsibility of management to establish an improvement culture and to ensure that the continuous improvement process works in practice. Management needs to set a good example and lead the way. If management begins to work with continuous improvements as part of its own practice, it will often trickle down through the rest of the organization. This is where many managers discover that they need to change how they work. They may not possess all the competencies needed to take a systematic approach to the improvement process. It is usually possible to postpone operational problems without too much trouble. But what is new in a lean culture is that the manager needs to ensure progress in both operations and improvement activities in order to appear credible.

In our experience, managers need to learn to define assignments more precisely. When a company works with continuous improvements, there are many tasks in progress at the same time. The manager therefore needs to be able to delegate well-defined tasks to avoid being overrun by follow-up activities. In practical terms, defining a task precisely means being able to work with the purpose of an assignment as well as its success criteria, end deliverables and sub-deliverables, agreed budget, timetable and planning. This is a critical competency for a manager in a knowledge-based organization. And yet, it is often the employees who receive training in this area over several days, while the managers, themselves, only set aside a couple of hours for a briefing. It is, in fact, a key management tool that managers unfortunately often choose to barely touch upon.

Improving Management Efficiency

For managers, it is relevant to take a long, hard look at themselves to find out how the management processes can be improved. This gives the managers experience with identifying and implementing improvement opportunities. The introduction of lean will usually be a welcome opportunity to harmonize and coordinate the management philosophy with real-life operations – something that most managers can appreciate.

Most companies are not very consistent in their management practices, despite the fact that most managers face the same challenges across the organization. In many cases, practice is based on a set of overall values and a few budget and reporting processes. As additional support, the managers may be offered further training as needed in personal development, coaching, difficult interviews etc. This is all very good, but how managers perceive management and the style of management they practice is often left up to the individual to decide. There is an enormous freedom to choose the approach that best suits the individual. This can seem like a kind of 'civil right' and is, in many ways, a very positive thing. However, we have met managers who are not particularly good at formulating their management tasks or who feel that they have been left on their own with their management responsibilities. They both want and need more opportunities to discuss with their colleagues how they can be better leaders. Management is a work process to the power of two. The question is how can you, as a manager, be a better leader and have more energy to support the knowledge work in your management area?

When we discuss this theme with managers, they are often concerned that standardization in management will be unhealthy for the company – that it can become too claustrophobic, too top-down and too deliberate. This is interesting, because huge sums are spent on designing strategies for the company and on process improvements in general. So why should the management, which is what stands between the strategies and the employees, remain an 'uncultivated' area? Establishing efficiency at that level would, in fact, generate great value.

Of course, variety should still be maintained by establishing processes that challenge and renew common practice.

We only have positive experiences with managers who gladly begin talking to each other about how they behave as leaders, and we often see managers participate with great interest and commitment.

But how do we prioritize?

Most managers discover that increased focus on continuous improvements forces them to devote less attention to other tasks and to develop their management skills. There are things they used to do that they will simply no longer have time for if they are to spend more time developing and streamlining the organization through continuous improvements. This is an improvement in itself, because many of the old tasks do not create nearly as much value for customers. It may be helpful to make a list of the manager's current responsibilities and then a list of the tasks he or she will no longer handle in future.

Visible and Active Leadership

In general, managers find that a lean innovation process brings them closer to a more visible and active leadership role. By leadership, we mean the way you maintain a close dialog with your employees about the organization's objectives and improvements, which can lead to a better and more competitive company. Managers will discover that they become more process-oriented, both in their own departments and across the departments, and thereby come closer to the employees in the customer-oriented processes.

As they implement continuous improvements, managers will begin tapping into new skills within themselves. They will become more systematic in how they practice leadership, they will share experiences with their colleagues and it will be easier for everyone to see what decisions have been made and whether they are carried out. All in all, there are many opportunities to develop your approach to management and your practical leadership skills by seeking inspiration in the lean principles for the benefit of the company, the customers and the employees.

When Management Becomes a Strategic Competency

Companies that have worked with lean management as a central leadership philosophy for a number of years will find that it can be difficult to recruit managers from the outside who do not have experience with lean.

ECCO, which has worked with lean at management level and throughout the organization for a number of years, shares this experience. According to Jens Christian Meier, EVP for production and logistics, the company has found it increasingly difficult to recruit managers from the outside because the investments that are made in lean would be lost if the managers taking over a new area are not acquainted with the management practice developed over the years. It can also be difficult at senior management level to find people who are able and willing to adapt to the management practice that has been developed and implemented over time.

Often, you do not realize how much a company has changed until you try to bring managers in from the outside who do not share the same philosophy.

Examples of Lean in Management

In the following, we will present a few specific solutions that management teams in various companies have introduced as a consequence of working with lean in management. The examples we have chosen to highlight are:

- Improvement boards at management level
- Standardization of management practice
- Zone management

Hopefully the examples will serve as inspiration for how lean can be implemented. Of course, you may not be able to use them directly, because there are major differences from company to company when it comes to organization, project type, maturity etc.

Improvement Boards at Management Level

This is a method that helps managers increase the commitment and participation of their employees. The method also establishes a system for working with continuous improvements. You can work with continuous improvements in a variety of ways, but if you want to maintain the new behavior, it is a good idea to establish some regular routines.

The figure below shows an example of an improvement board. The improvement board, which should be hung up in a central location in the department, can be made in various ways and is a place where the employees can continuously post improvement ideas. The department gathers around the board on a regular basis, for example once a week, to celebrate ideas that have been implemented, prioritize improvement ideas and decide which new initiatives to launch. At these meetings, the manager can summarize the department's targets and evaluate what has been achieved.

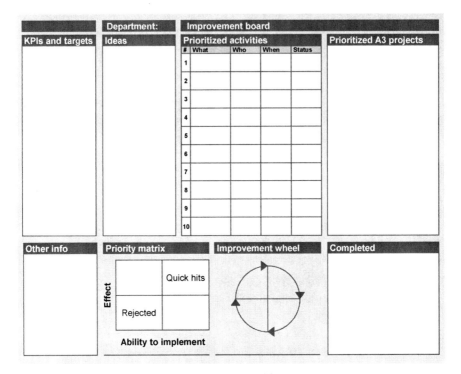

Figure 5.5. Improvement Board for Management and Support

The board meeting follows a set agenda and should only take 20-40 minutes. It is not a time for discussing solutions or how problems can be solved. An idea is only discussed long enough to be able to prioritize it and to decide the appropriate action.

Some of the improvement ideas will be so comprehensive that they cannot be immediately implemented by one or two people over the next two weeks. In such cases, a project description should be drawn up to form the basis for a decision the following week.

Commitment to Doing Something

The improvement board is a powerful symbol that the department or the company is working with lean. But this, of course, is not a goal in itself. The primary aim is to establish a process of continuous improvements that results in the efficient execution of tasks. Improvement boards help make the common goals more visible and get the employees involved and committed to contributing to the visions of the organization. It promotes pride and excellence in the organization and ensures simplified and consequent follow-up on the improvement initiatives that are started up.

When a manager introduces an improvement board, it is a commitment. It is highly visible and everyone can see the manager's good intentions. The positive thing about working with an improvement board is that it acts as an anchor for the improvement initiatives. The manager can visibly show his or her commitment to the improvement culture. It may sound like the improvement board has a purely symbolic value. This is far from true. If the manager is able to maintain the routine and integrate the board meetings naturally into his or her management process, a variety of valuable improvements can actually be achieved. However, this presumes that the manager is able to facilitate the process around the board in a positive manner.

The Manager Must be a Facilitator

There are many aspects that help facilitate meetings around the board in a positive atmosphere. The manager needs to be able to stand up in front of the employees and facilitate the process, ask questions, listen and motivate. It is important to motivate the employees to come with suggestions and to manage the suggestions by prioritizing them and finally deciding to implement them. Facilitating the meetings is a management responsibility. The organization's time and resources are allocated at the meeting. It is an important management instrument, but it must take place in mutual understanding with the employees. Imagine a situation where the manager stands in front of the board and rejects an employee's idea without discussion. That can seriously affect the employee's desire to present ideas in the future.

The meetings in front of the board can also be used to discuss the organization's strategy and targets as well as progress in relation to achieving them. Target setting and follow up is an important part of the meetings, where you can discuss what it will take to achieve the goals or why the organization's results deviate from the set targets. In this way, the manager can use the improvement board to link strategies, current practice and improvement initiatives.

Linking Improvement Boards

Improvement boards can be linked across the company, allowing improvement ideas to be moved from one board to another. This can take place both horizontally and vertically. It is normal for an improvement idea to be moved up in the organization if implementing the idea requires a solution in several areas at the same time. For instance, an employee might suggest that materials should be received from a different department than what has otherwise been standard procedure. This idea could be moved to an improvement board in the department responsible for those materials, because they are the ones who need to address it.

It is important that the manager understands that employees might come with a lot of improvement ideas which fall outside their own area. It is generally easier to see what others should do differently than what you could do yourself. This movement can actually be quite helpful because it provides an outside perspective on things. However, it may, at some point, be necessary to encourage the employees to contribute more ideas that fall within their own area of operations. This trains their ability to reflect on the best way to do things, and makes it much easier to start introducing changes in their own area. There is a lot to be learned from identifying, developing and implementing changes.

Many Improvements

It is difficult to make changes and stick to them, especially if you introduce a lot of changes within a short time span. Thinking about continuous improvement can result in so many consecutive changes that it can be difficult to follow up on all the new initiatives. It is therefore vital that the manager makes sure the introduced improvements are also manageable.

It is important not to be too idealistic about the changes you introduce. We have seen examples of companies that have introduced a long line of rules for how work should be done based on good intentions. But do not forget to be critical. You should question whether the improvements that have been introduced really create value and whether the way they have been introduced is actually sustainable.

Improvements shouldn't be something you introduce 'because you are working with lean'. Improvements should only be introduced because they make sense in the given situation. You can introduce solutions, only to realize after a while that they have not had the desired effect or that they are difficult to maintain. If something does not work after a period of time, you need to ask what is wrong. Maybe it can be an item on the improvement board: Is it too difficult? Has there been a failure in communication? Are we too impatient?

There can be a variety of reasons, but it is all part of developing how you work – some things will work, some things will need to be adjusted and some things simply will not work, regardless of how good the idea was. And remember, it is important to remove anything that does not work – always tidy up. It is okay to experiment and to learn. But not tidying up is a sign that the entire process has gone off track.

The manager is responsible for ensuring that the agreed changes are implemented. Lean is about establishing more consistency in your actions. If you have decided to launch an initiative on a specific date – then keep that date. If you regret having introduced an initiative – then cancel it. It is okay to learn from your mistakes, and doing so also avoids wasting further resources.

The Number of Improvements

Along these same lines, it can also be a good idea to keep the number of concurrent improvement activities at a minimum, bearing in mind the principle of one-piece flow. The whole point of continuous improvements is that they are continuous. The manager should plan consumption of the organization's energy like a marathon runner. The best approach is a slow and steady process.

Some managers stick to the principle of having only five or, maximum, ten initiatives in progress at a time. And new initiatives may not be introduced until something has been completed. For some organizations, lean helps focus the improvement process, thus dramatically reducing the number of concurrent improvement initiatives.

The Scope of Improvements

Another important aspect is the scope of the improvements and, especially, the time it takes to develop and implement them. The best approach when starting up a continuous improvement culture is to implement improvements that are not too time and resource consuming.

If you are too ambitious, you run the risk of it becoming a chore and loosing the momentum. Remember, building up routines for identifying and maintaining improvements is a learning process.

It creates motivation if you are able to celebrate successes at regular intervals. A good pace is to begin with initiatives that can be implemented within a couple of weeks. This creates flow in the improvement process. If you like, you can alternate between smaller and larger initiatives.

Keeping the Improvement Process Alive

Keeping the improvement process alive over time is a management challenge that requires perseverance. It often helps to make the improvement board a routine. It is also a good idea to decide that the improvement process should proceed, even if the manager is out of office on that particular day. A good way to keep the improvement process running smoothly is for the manager to share the responsibility with one or two others.

People are generally very enthusiastic about the process when it is first introduced. They come up with lots of good ideas – big and small. Many employees feel like they finally have a way to call attention to potential improvement areas. A channel they have wanted access to for a long time is suddenly available. It can feel like the floodgates have been opened, and it is not uncommon to see 50 improvement ideas on the board after the first meeting. There is a positive energy, and the manager feels like everything is going smoothly. But this is where it is a good idea to look forward in the process, because receiving a lot of improvement ideas is often not a problem. The real challenge is doing something about the suggestions. This is where it helps to choose ideas that are not too big and not too small and that can be implemented immediately.

After a while, the flow of new ideas will begin to ebb. It obviously becomes more difficult to find something new, many think. But this is only partly true. Because if the process works well, there will always be something that can be improved. It is inconceivable that everything has been optimized and that there is nothing left to do. This is where it is important that the manager insists on having something to work with and gets it on the board.

One way to do this is to give every meeting a theme, i.e. to choose a theme for the kinds of improvement ideas you are looking for. For example, you can decide to focus on customer relations one week, internal cooperation or documentation the next and so forth. The possibilities are endless.

In some management areas, the distance between the employees' specializations and their current work area is so great that it can be difficult for employees to know whether their improvement ideas actually belong on the board. They wonder whether something they personally consider a problem is also relevant to the rest of the group. This is problematic because we are just as interested in the little improvements. One solution could be to break up the group, placing employees with natural relationships together in smaller groups and then having them work with improvement ideas.

Creation of value is a huge motivating factor. The improvement process can lose some of its momentum if introduced initiatives have not been completed or if it is unclear what value they create.

The Manager's Experience

When we talk to managers who have introduced improvement boards, one of the first things they usually say is that everything is going perfectly and that lean really makes sense. But many overlook one element: In order for the improvements to work, the manager needs to change his or her management focus and make the necessary prioritizations. The manager has not yet realized that lean is a philosophy, because the tool is working just fine. If it were possible, at this point, to make the manager see that this is not enough, then things would look even better.

The problem is that working with improvements is not just something that takes place on the improvement boards alone. During the week prior to the meeting, the manager needs to ask the employees how the new initiatives are working out, whether they need any adjustments and how they can be communicated and maintained. This is where the manager plays a particularly important role as coach; a role that takes time and the right competencies.

Clear Ownership of Processes and Methods

One way to significantly reduce the complexity of implementing continuous improvements is to ensure clear and unambiguous ownership of the key processes and methods. This has proven an effective method for handling large numbers of improvements. Processes and methods in a knowledge-based organization can be viewed as an infrastructure that needs to be developed and maintained just like the physical environment.

For every process or method, someone should be appointed responsible for developing and maintaining them. That way, when someone proposes an improvement, everyone knows exactly who is responsible for receiving and handling the suggestion.

Central processes and methods can include the overall model for project implementation, methods for customer involvement, IT tools, training, templates for documentation, QA systems and evaluation methods.

In a modern knowledge-based company, many processes and methods are introduced for the purpose of supporting and facilitating the knowledge work. Employees often perceive these initiatives as negative, resource demanding and tiresome. That's not how it is supposed to be. And if that is how people feel, then it should lead to an improvement idea so the person responsible for methods can do something about it.

Standardizing Management Practice

Standardizing is another way to increase the ability to handle a large number of changes. To a lot of people, the word 'standardization' has a negative ring to it. But standardization can also be a way to focus your mental capacity on those aspects that produce the most value by automatizing simple processes.

In fact, according to Taiichi Ohno: "If there is no standard – there can be no kaizen." It is hard to implement continuous improvements without a method for maintaining the level you have reached. But how do you do that? Standardization in knowledge environments has many aspects. For instance, speaking a common language is a kind of standardization, so are check lists and method descriptions.

Even though many have a negative attitude towards standardization, there are plenty of examples of the positive effect standardization can have. The secret may be that good standardizations go unnoticed, while standardizations that do not work practically shout out at us. The challenge we then face is to find the standardizations that make our work easier. Good standardizations do not need to be enforced. They become a natural part of the work flow. Standardization is a way to simplify things so we can continue to make the work even easier for ourselves.

Coordinated Meeting Structure

A standardized management practice can be used to streamline management work. The idea is that management agrees on how to perform a specific management task, and then introduces a method for everyone to follow. In a knowledge-based company, for instance, where a large share of the work is organized into projects, it may be relevant to coordinate the meeting structure to ensure that departmental meetings, monthly meetings and other types of meetings do not turn the project process into an obstacle course.

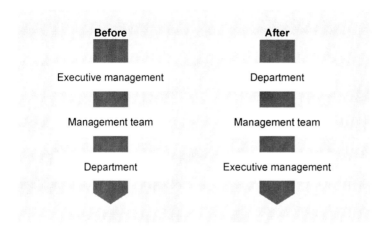

Figure 5.6. Organizing Meeting Flow

A coordinated meeting structure can be used to facilitate the lean culture. In many companies, for example, management meetings tend to be organized in the same way, with meetings at the highest level taking place early in the work week, followed by meetings at lower levels, and, finally, the individual employees are informed about the decisions that have been made. In the following figure, this structure is represented by the flow on the left.

The structure represented on the right supports an improvement culture. It starts with the individual areas closest to the employees, i.e. improvement board meetings. These are followed by meetings at the next level, and finally the meetings at the highest level are held. This structure focuses on operations. It allows improvement ideas from operations to travel through the management structure and be processed. This, then, allows decisions to be made to implement initiatives that support what the individual employees close to the value-creating process are working with. Even for minor initiatives, this approach signals that management are willing to make changes to improve efficiency.

Zone Management

The principle of appointing one person to be responsible for large portions of the organization's infrastructure can also be implemented at management level. In the example presented in the following figure, a management team has chosen to divide the various areas up among them. There are three overall areas: operations, development and follow-up.

	Operations		Development		Follow-up/QA	
Process	Project process	Department process	Cross-functional improvements	Training	Audit	KPI's
Owner	SFN	TMI	CS	LK	SAL	HSO
Content	Project manual	Resource management Board meetings Department process VSM	Portfolio management: Cross-organizational improvement projects	Lean courses	Project manager audit	KPI system

Figure 5.7. Establishing Cross-organizational Process Responsibility with Management Zones

'Operations' covers the processes and methods affiliated with the daily work processes in the organization, such as the overall project model, capacity, staffing and departmental improvement processes. 'Development', in this context, covers the cross-organizational improvement projects and training (streamlining a knowledge-based organization often involves a good deal of training). The third area, 'follow-up', concentrates on the measurement and incentive system as well as the QA system.

The above division was developed at Ramboll Oil & Gas, where the work processes have strategic importance. The managers in this example each have a cross-organizational responsibility in addition to their key role as department manager for between 20 and 50 employees.

Generally, the principle of making managers responsible for cross-organizational processes alongside their own departmental responsibilities is a good idea for several reasons: Firstly, focus is concentrated on the cross-organizational processes that would otherwise have a tendency to be everyone's responsibility and thus no one's. Improvement ideas for cross-organizational processes have a recipient, and responsibility for maintaining and developing them is clearly placed. Secondly, division into management zones increases the managers' understanding of the cross-functional interaction that takes place because their responsibilities span every department. It is often the employees who work across the entire organization, because they participate in the projects, while the managers generally operate within their own departments and only optimize within their own area.

Zone management makes it legitimate at management level to become involved in each others' departments and to suggest how the company as a whole can make its work more efficient. It also encourages people to take a more constructive approach to the problems that can develop between departments. Zone management can be used to increase the managers' awareness and ability to work with the processes. It is also a good opportunity to form a high-performing management team.

Management Must Take the Lead

Lean is about management, and obviously when trying to change a company's culture, management need to lead the way. This can be extremely difficult for some managers. But having the support of colleagues and being able to share experiences makes the process much easier.

We find that lean works well as a common management project and is a good way to bring managers in an organization closer together. They agree to work together towards a common objective: to push the boundaries for management and create a new and visibly different culture within the company.

To take the lead, management can start with two things: First, the entire management team needs to figure out how to simplify and streamline the management practices based on the lean principles. Second, they need to decide how to behave towards their employees and how to work together to ensure that the corporate culture continue moving in the right direction.

Literature:

Covey, Stephen R.: The 7 Habits of Highly Effective People – Powerful Lessons in Personal Change. Free Press, 1989.

DeLong, Thomas J., Gabarro, John J., Lees, Robert J.: *When Professionals Have to Lead – A New Model for High Performance*. Harvard Business School Press, 2007.

Hamel, Gary: *The Future of Management*. Harvard Business Press, 2007.

Hamel, Gary: "Moon Shots for Management". Harvard Business Review, 2009.

Maister, David H.: "Are You Ready for Practice Group Leaders". 1999, http://davidmaister.com/articles/1/34/.

Maister, David H: "A Matter of Trust". 2005, http://davidmaister.com/articles/2/25/.

Maister, David H., Galford, Robert M., Green, Charles H.: *The Trusted Advisor*. Simon & Schuster, 2001.

Scharmer, Otto C.: *Theory U: Learning From the Future as It Emerges*. Berrett Kohler Publishers Inc., San Francisco, 2009.

Chapter 6
Realizing Your Strategy through Portfolio Management

Portfolio management is an often-overlooked discipline for promoting efficiency in the innovation process. Portfolio management is a method for creating a framework that fosters focus and progress in the projects. However, portfolio management often becomes too advanced, and the good intentions drown in prioritization models, prioritization reports and unclear future plans. This does not alter the fact that good portfolio management is a prerequisite for creating the best possible project conditions. Using lean in portfolio management means being inspired by the lean principles to create simple and healthy conditions for project work.

Organizing Knowledge Work into Projects

A few years ago, we visited a company that had organized their innovation process as a flow of cases in a line organization comprising technical departments. For instance, a case might involve developing a new software module for a remote reading unit. The development organization had a staff of approx. 260 people, including 33 managers and seven organizational levels.

A central planning office was responsible for breaking down the assignments into cases, which were then sent to the respective departments to be processed under the management and control of the heads of the technical departments. Each case was solved locally and then sent back to the planning office where all the solutions were compiled and sent to production for further processing.

To many people, conducting innovation work in a line organization with centralized planning might seem bureaucratic and antiquated. And the company did have problems with lead times and quality, despite the hard work of line managers. The projects took a long time, and no one could anticipate when they would all be finished. The employees' desks were piled high with files. Many of the problems with the quality of the solutions were caused by poor coordination. For example, one department might decide that their equipment should be mounted on a wall, while another department recommended that it be removed.

C. Sehested, H. Sonnenberg, *Lean Innovation,* DOI 10.1007/978-3-642-15895-7_7,
© Springer-Verlag Berlin Heidelberg 2011

Most knowledge-based organizations choose to work in projects. It makes sense because the tasks require collaboration and coordination among a number of specialists. One person – the project manager (in conjunction with the project team) – is responsible for ensuring that the project delivers the promised results at the agreed time. But organizing innovation work more appropriately into projects does not eliminate the need for management.

An important job for the management is to prioritize which projects to implement and to establish healthy conditions for those projects. The management team is responsible for making the best possible use of the employees' competencies. Management and coordination of the company's potential, current projects and resources form the core of project portfolio management – or simply portfolio management.

The Management Must Be Committed to the Portfolio

Unfortunately, many companies do not give portfolio management the attention it deserves. Generally, the line management participates in the prioritization process, but their primary responsibility tends to be for their own focus areas. It is often unclear who is responsible for ensuring that the portfolio management process functions satisfactorily across the entire organization, and who, besides the managing director, is responsible for handling any problems that might result from improper portfolio management. This should be enough to motivate the managing director to ensure a clear and unambiguous distribution of responsibilities and to ensure that the portfolio is managed properly.

Employees in a knowledge-based organization spend most of their time on projects and are only back in the line functions for very short periods to 'refuel'. The purpose of portfolio management is to:

• Realize the company's strategy
• Allocate resources to the most important initiatives
• Create efficiency in projects
• Apply employee capabilities efficiently
• Ensure coordination between the projects and avoid duplicated effort

The quality of portfolio management affects the employees, the customers and the technical development. Poor portfolio management can result in all kinds of problems: projects may be delayed, employees may be shifted from project to project, resources end up going to whatever seems most urgent but not necessarily most important etc.

Portfolio Management – A Learning Process

There is always too much to do in a knowledge-based organization – or at least the opposite is very rarely the case. Normally, the demand for innovation is greater than the available resources. Therefore it is also important to have an understanding of the organizational capacity and to be good at prioritizing the projects and tasks you decide to initiate. If everyone is very busy it can be a problem, but it is also a positive situation. The good ideas should fight for resources. If there are not enough good ideas, you risk implementing bad ideas just to have something to do, and that would be unfortunate.

Prioritization should happen before work on the projects begins. And no one can work on more than one thing at a time. Consequently, if management initiates projects without thinking them through, the employees can end up having to prioritize their work themselves. And that can develop into chaos, wasting both time and resources. Prioritization should therefore take place early in the process.

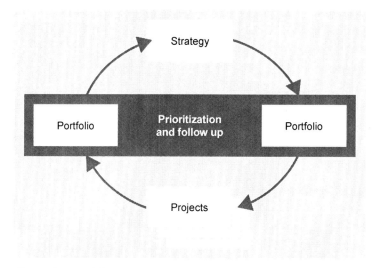

Figure 6.1. Portfolio Management as a Management and Learning Loop

The above model shows the connection between strategy, portfolio management and projects. The strategy is translated via portfolio management into a series of projects. There is regular follow-up on the portfolio throughout the process, and adjustments are made. Portfolio management can be viewed as a management and learning loop according to the same model as continuous improvements (Plan-Do-Check-Act).

Portfolio management is based on the company's strategies and represents a prioritization and control layer in relation to the individual projects that are initiated. When you compare the company's current position with its strategy, the project portfolio is the difference between the two. The above model can be used to bring portfolio management up to the strategic level where it belongs. Portfolio management is clearly a management task. And management is responsible for ensuring that the prioritization is not too short-sighted.

Even though we recommend executing portfolio management at a strategic level, this does not mean that only strategic projects are to be prioritized. Successful portfolio management is about striking a balance between the short and the long term. It is like balancing on a bicycle while at the same time trying to get where you want to go. You cannot prioritize one thing without also being aware of the other. The most important management tasks associated with portfolio management are:

- Matching portfolio management with project type
- Ensuring a healthy portfolio that creates value
- Prioritizing projects for start-up
- Establishing a framework that promotes progress
- Optimizing resources and staffing projects
- Portfolio follow-up and fine-tuning

These management tasks will be explored in more detail in the following sections.

Matching Portfolio Management with Project Type

Large-scale, cross-organizational projects and small local projects are often carried out at the same time in the same organization with the same employees. This makes portfolio management difficult. Obtaining an overview of every project currently in progress in a knowledge-based organization can seem overwhelming. Different types of organizations following different business models handle customer-oriented projects differently.

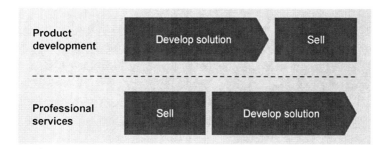

Figure 6.2. Push and Pull Business Models

The business model on top is a 'push model' where the solution is developed before it is sold. The model on the bottom is a 'pull model' where the solution is sold before it is developed.

The business model affects how we work with portfolio management. The push model is typical for product/service development in traditional manufacturing companies. Such companies have a large number of projects they can choose to initiate, making portfolio management a matter of prioritization based on a slightly longer perspective. In the pull model, portfolio management is primarily about finding the capacity to carry out the projects that are sold. This model is typical for professional service companies like law firms, advertising agencies and consultancies.

However, there are also many in-between types. For instance, a manufacturing company may also offer a service such as product modifications based on specific customer requests. Similarly, service companies may work with conceptualizing new services. This is the key to understanding the problems many companies have with portfolio management; the project portfolio is usually a combination of many types of projects.

Ensuring a Healthy Portfolio that Creates Value

Healthy and value-creating portfolio management requires a good overview of the work being carried out in the organization. For many organizations, the best starting point is to obtain an overview of all the projects in progress across the entire organization. This can be done by making a list of all current projects.

Opinions about the projects often differ, so making several rounds of the organization may be necessary to get a complete picture of what everyone is currently working on. Sometimes it can be difficult to determine whether the list is exhaustive. In such cases, it can help to stop work on anything that is not on the list.

In one company, drawing up and presenting just such a project list led to a discussion about a project involving 12 people. Apparently, the project had been stopped more than two years ago because it had no future. What a wonderful gift! Suddenly, 12 people were freed up to work on other projects. Eliminating work which no one has requested is a simple way to reduce waste.

There are many ways to maintain an overview of the portfolio. The project list will usually be created in Excel or Word. However, these lists should contain only the information necessary to enable a team discussion and nothing more. Furthermore, they should strengthen the common vision of the management team. This is not possible with a 700-row spreadsheet all in font size 6.

Alternatively, you can use 'visual management' or *oobeya* as Toyota calls it. This is a room where visual plans are hung up on the walls, showing the projects in relation to each other. It is a kind of 'portfolio war room'.

Figure 6.3. Portfolio War Room

The most important challenges in the portfolio are posted on boards. The room is filled with project objectives, risk matrices and prototypes. This helps the projects 'climb' out of the spreadsheets, making them easier to understand. This insight leads to better decision-making as well as increased ownership and more energy from the management. It helps visualize the shared dream at the end of the portfolio. Another way to achieve an overview of the project portfolio is by taking a closer look at how resources are used in the various types of projects.

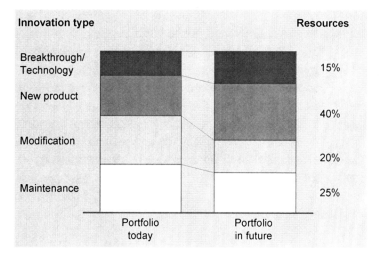

Figure 6.4. Portfolio Planning with Resource Pools

Based on the project list, the projects are grouped into types as illustrated in the above figure. This makes it possible to compare the actual resource consumption with the resource allocation considered ideal for the company and consistent with its strategy. This type of analysis usually reveals that the resource consumption does not reflect the desired distribution.

Typically, there are too many short-term projects in the portfolio and not enough focus on the long-term perspective. When we ask why this is, we are often told that minor modifications and maintenance tasks tend to be given higher priority because the projects are both well defined and relatively urgent in nature. In general, working on the wrong projects because of improper portfolio planning must be considered waste.

Prioritizing Projects for Start-up

Once you have an overview of the strategy and of how you want to allocate your resources, the next question is how to choose which projects to start. It is crucial that people are working on the right tasks. And the judges of that – the project customers – can be both external and internal. When making prioritizations within the portfolio, the evaluation can be based on three types of criteria or on a combination of them. The three types are:

1. Strategy criteria: These are long-term and future-oriented prioritizations. For example, you might choose to prioritize a project to develop new

services for the German market to support a planned expansion into Germany for strategic reasons. There may not be a business case to document that the project is profitable, but the project is important for supporting the company's strategy.

2. Value criteria: These are prioritizations based on the value you expect to generate by implementing the project. Value is normally considered from a financial point of view. However, value can also be based on other criteria, such as environmental impact or employee satisfaction.

3. Balance criteria: It is important to have a strong portfolio which utilizes the resources efficiently. Say you want to ensure balance in the project with regard to risks, duration or employee workload. To do this, the management team can choose to prioritize a project because it utilizes resources that would otherwise be lost.

Various types of objective decision frameworks can be developed. For instance, projects can be given points for how well they meet specific criteria. However any assessment, regardless of method, will ultimately be subjective in practice. But being aware of the three perspectives can make it more legitimate to express different points of view before deciding what to prioritize.

In practice, people tend to end up in either one camp or the other. The arguments in favor of projects are either because they are strategically important or because they have a positive and immediate impact on the bottom line. And it can be difficult to give projects equal treatment. But it is necessary to develop the ability to prioritize and implement projects based on all three perspectives. The portfolio should be inspiring to work with. It is the company's ticket to the future. Consequently, working with the portfolio must never become mindless planning.

The projects that are ready for start-up should be so attractive that everyone has an interest in finishing up their current projects as quickly as possible. To reach this point, try releasing yourself from the existing portfolio and imagine how you would compose the portfolio if you could start over – then ask yourself and each other: Is there something we could do differently?

Establishing a Framework that Promotes Progress

Another purpose of portfolio management is to define a framework for projects in order to give them a boost and help them reach their goals. Using the lean principles will enable you to achieve an entirely new level of portfolio management.

Healthy framework for projects

Few projects

Short lead time

High staffing ratio

100% resources

Fixed timeframe

Uniform takt for all projects

Simple visual overview

Figure 6.5. Lean Principles in Portfolio Management

In the following, we will show how the lean principles can inspire you to think outside the box when it comes to composing and managing a portfolio of innovation projects. The above table lists some of the principles that work well in our experience.

Portfolio Management with One-Piece Flow

We have previously referred to companies' lack of project prioritization. This is a difficult process, and often they end up having too many ongoing projects at once. It is, therefore, a good principle to complete one project at a time. In practice, this will often mean initiating fewer projects at the same time, but with a larger team on each project. This increases the intensity of the projects. In the following figure, this corresponds to moving from portfolio A to portfolio B.

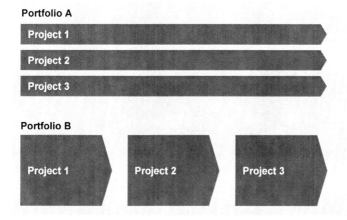

Figure 6.6. Two Principles for Organizing Project Portfolios

This has the added advantage of reducing the duration of the project, which means you can learn from the project more quickly. And that knowledge can be put to use in the next project. This gives you a higher pace of continuous improvements, a steeper learning curve and increases the level of professionalism.

We have talked about the importance of a simple and manageable portfolio. For instance, reducing the number of projects by 50 per cent will result in better utilization of resources, and management will divide its attention among less projects. The goal is to make the innovation portfolio more lean. Running a focused portfolio is both lean and smart. It ensures that enough resources are allocated to individual projects, which help keep a high level of innovativeness and complete the project on time, so you can move on.

Strictly speaking, the ideal lean state is one-piece flow. One-piece flow reduces the work in progress. This is because it costs money from a project starts until the results are available, and from the product is put into production until it is shipped out to the stores. And these costs can add up quickly. In the following figure, portfolio A shows an investment of six employees over 12 months before any return on that investment is seen, while in portfolio B the investment is six employees over just four months. Financially, there is a huge difference.

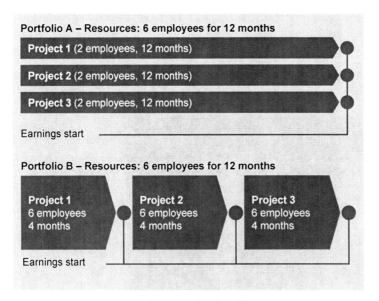

Figure 6.7. One-piece Flow Generates Earnings Faster

The math can be even more attractive if it is based on the business potential of the projects rather than on investments in man-months. This can have a significant impact on the company's bottom line.

In some types of knowledge work and sectors, a project cannot be finished within six or 12 months. And if the project is in a brand new field, it can be very difficult to predict how long it will take to finish. However, a professional knowledge-based organization should have an ambition to transform knowledge into value as fast as possible.

Portfolio Management with Timeboxing

The lean principle of timeboxing is perfectly suited portfolio management. If it is difficult to keep a project within the defined timeframe, the problems should be solved by reducing the scope of the project or by adding more resources.

LINAK, which manufactures electrical linear actuators, divides projects into categories based on an assessment of resource needs, finances and risks. The projects and resources then have to be adapted to the time that is available. Sometimes, it is necessary to reduce the project's level of ambition to fit it into the timeframe.

If a project comes under time pressure, it can aim to develop a basic model which has been modified to meet a reduced set of specifications. This model can then be upgraded and features can be added later.

When developing health care products, Coloplast uses timeboxing in its projects. According to John Raabo Nielsen, SVP for R&D, one of their divisions recently completed three projects according to this principle. Two of the projects were timeboxed to six months, while the third was timeboxed to nine months. Coloplast found that this approach produced a good flow and that it fostered a high level of creativity in the project teams.

The advantage of timeboxing, in John Nielsen's view, is increased focus on the project. Anything problematic in the project comes to the surface almost immediately. Furthermore, the project team expects management to make fast and efficient decisions. As a result, the steering committee became better at managing the projects and John Nielsen established better contact with the project teams.

Reducing development time and increasing staffing is generally a good idea. Reducing development time is like lowering the water level in a lake. Things that do not work properly immediately become visible and it is possible to solve them once and for all.

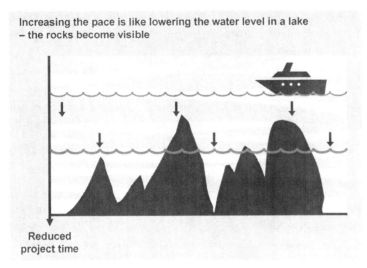

Increasing the pace is like lowering the water level in a lake
– the rocks become visible

Reduced
project time

Figure 6.8. Reduced Development Time Reveals Waste

Conditions that can be revealed by reducing development time include delayed documentation tasks, slow approval procedures, a lack of standard working methods, insufficient intensity in the project process etc.

The primary outcome of reducing development time is increased efficiency – the project participants simply grew more focused throughout the process. This increases the company's ability to react more quickly to new opportunities and threats in the market.

Portfolio Management with Takt

Takt is about maintaining a steady frequency in the deliverables so you can regularly and consistently generate the results that are expected. The purpose of takt is to ensure progress, level out the resource load and increase trust by keeping your promises.

For instance, in order to supply four new products per year, you need to deliver a product every three months. If each project is timeboxed to six months, you need to have two projects in progress concurrently. This type of purely mathematical logic can be valuable in the effort to simplify portfolio management.

Takt can be used to prioritize the portfolio by creating a launch calendar. A launch calendar is a good way to visualize expectations about the degree of novelty and number of solutions that the knowledge organization is expected to deliver.

Innovation type	Year							
	0	1	2	3	4	5	6	7
Breakthrough/ Technology	X				X			
New product	X		X		X		X	
Modification	X	X		X	X		X	
Maintenance	X	X	X	X	X	X	X	X

Figure 6.9. Portfolio Management with a Launch Calendar

The launch calendar can be based on the strategy or current market needs. At the time the launch calendar is created, you may not know exactly what the projects involve. But that is okay. The knowledge workers and the management can define that at a later stage.

One way a launch calendar can establish takt in the portfolio is by ensuring that the dialog with internal stakeholders regarding needs and expectations is initiated early in the process. This makes it easier to estimate capacity and competency needs. A launch calendar also provides a good overview, creating breathing room to help focus more energy on the contents of the solutions. This allows the organization to respond faster to deviations because everyone can clearly see whether the organization is maintaining its takt.

Takt can also be a way for the employees to work. Projects develop a regular rhythm so everyone knows what needs to be finished and when. It is like a symphony orchestra, where the takt regulates the input of the various musicians. You know exactly where everyone else is and where you are – and you can concentrate on perfecting your own contribution. This gives you more time to focus on the content of the deliverable.

In some companies, the takt will naturally be set by external obligations, such as seasons, trade fairs etc. In other companies, it will be necessary to establish an artificial takt. LINAK has introduced a takt where projects may only be completed at the end of a quarter. This has established a project period of at least three months. The advantage is that it calls attention to and instills respect for deadlines. According to the principle, if a project exceeds the quarterly deadline, it cannot be submitted for approval until the next product committee meeting three months later. One objective of these 'time slots' has been to give the department breathing room, with fewer reprioritizations and resource allocations in their daily operations.

The introduction of takt at LINAK, which put an end to the practice of completing projects ad hoc, also had the unexpected positive effect that every quarter large numbers of employees were freed up all at once for other work. This promotes much more strategic portfolio management because enough employees are freed up to initiate larger and more challenging projects.

You might be wondering whether changing the takt time from every month to every quarter really is lean. A takt time of a month would clearly be preferable. The more you can reduce the planning horizon, the greater are your chances of getting it right, making your company both stronger and more flexible. In the above case, it was a matter of getting people to respect the deadline, and to do this they had to establish the necessary discipline. But takt time may subsequently be reduced even further.

Optimizing Project Resources and Staffing

People and projects are the key ingredients for producing results in a knowledge organization.

To improve efficiency, it is important that the management works with the two perspectives of people management: capacity and staffing.

- The capacity plan is the overall plan that shows the future resource needs for handling the expected quantity of work.
- The staffing plan is a detailed plan to ensure that the projects have the employees they need at their disposal.

Both capacity and staffing present special challenges in knowledge-based organizations. This is because specialists, in particular, are unique and cannot simply be replaced or substituted. Thus staffing is about organizing the work of these employees in the best possible way. Efficient resource planning requires that the project managers know at a very early stage which employees they will need and when. Therefore, project managers must be able to see the big picture.

At Exhausto, the project managers, production department, documentation department and the technical department meet every two weeks. At the meeting, which they have dubbed 'Combat Planning', they review a spreadsheet showing the next two weeks' resources, projects and days. The goal is to avoid bottlenecks in the next two weeks.

At Ramboll Oil & Gas, every team coordinates its resources on a weekly basis. The team gathers around a SmartBoard which interactively displays what everyone will be working on over the next few weeks. They discuss how to meet critical resource needs and how best to utilize any overcapacity.

Resource management is like all other aspects of lean: It works best with short, frequent meetings. In this context, simple tools that are intuitively easy to understand are often just as good as advanced IT tools. Many companies manage resources with the aid of a chart hung up on the wall featuring names, weeks and Post-its.

The ever-innovative design company, IDEO, takes resource management to the extreme. They do not have a committee to decide which projects the employees should work on. Instead, the projects compete with each other for the best resources. This is an advantage for projects with an inspiring vision, and it is a drawback for less attractive projects. IDEO has chosen this approach because motivated and enthusiastic employees are the key to their survival.

Portfolio Follow-up and Adjustment

Even though you prioritize your portfolio, it can be worthwhile to take a closer look at it on a regular basis to make sure that your initiatives are still relevant. It can also be helpful to maintain a dialog with the project teams. Do management and the project team still share the same view of the project?

Things rarely go as planned, and management is responsible for following up on the portfolio and adjusting it along the way. Continuous feedback from the projects is an important part of portfolio management. To work optimally, it is necessary to establish simple processes that require as few resources as possible. Management and the projects have to agree what kind of information the feedback should contain. And if the information can be based on something the project already 'produces', then a key source of waste can be eliminated.

Project managers often complain about requirements for documentation which they do not benefit from and which the management only rarely reacts to. In such situations, it can be a good idea to reconsider whether documentation tasks are the best way to use resources. With lean thinking, you might be able to find other, perhaps untraditional, solutions that create more value. For example, why doesn't the management go to the projects to hold steering committee meetings instead of the projects coming to the management? Why should the project record its progress in a database if the same information can be found in the project's visual plan which is hanging on the wall in the project room? The point is to think outside the box and to experiment with little changes, which, when combined, can generate significant value.

Measuring the Portfolio

Measurement is an important tool for determining project progress. It can be used by the management to communicate what is important and as a reward system. Project measurement is a key concept in lean. However, it must not be viewed as an external discipline creator, but rather as a way to understand progress and improve performance. It is actually built into many of the concepts, principles and methods that make up lean. Measurement in lean is generally driven by the people who actually have an influence on performance quality.

However, measurement in a knowledge-based organization can be a sensitive topic. It is therefore crucial that the thoughts behind performance and progress measurement and measurement-driven behavior in lean are properly communicated before the decision is made to introduce or expand measurement.

Many traditional measurement systems measure end results, such as meeting a deadline or the number of hours spent. To introduce project measurement in a lean culture, it is just as important to be able to conduct frequent continuous measurements on project status and intermediary results.

Canceling Projects

Sometimes it is necessary to cancel a project prematurely. Most top managers seem to agree on this. And yet, they seem to agree more in word than in action. Canceling a project is not that easy. Telling a project manager or a project team that something they have worked so hard on for the past six months was a waste of time and is being canceled is a hard thing to do.

But perhaps there is a better way to put it. Canceled projects or features are not wasted. While going on, they created motivation and generated relevant new knowledge. Is a prototype that never makes it to the market a waste? No; the purpose of a prototype is to generate learning for the project. A canceled project is only wasted if it did not generate learning for the portfolio. Ensuring the systematic flow of learning from canceled projects back into the portfolio could make canceling projects easier. At the beginning of an innovation project, you know very little, but you learn a lot along the way. You may even realize that you made a mistake. It is no one's fault; that is just the nature of knowledge work.

And there is always a middle course. There is also a solution somewhere between canceling a project and letting it continue. Google says, "Don't kill projects; morph them". In a very interesting YouTube video clip, Marissa Meyer talks about Google's approach to project portfolio adjustment. At Google, major projects are not always stopped, even though they receive a negative project evaluation. If a group of innovative people has been enthusiastic about an idea, it must contain some kind of value. There must be a reason for their enthusiasm. Maybe the idea or concept did not have the right conditions? Maybe a new approach is needed to rejuvenate the concept.

Examples of Lean in Portfolio Management

In the following, we would like to give some examples of ways companies have been inspired by lean to make portfolio management and capacity planning more efficient.

We will look at:

- Portfolio prioritization
- Portfolio overview as a horserace
- Measuring project focus and progress

It can be inspiring to see how other companies have developed internal portfolio and resource management processes so they facilitate their strategic ambitions and project objectives in the right way.

Portfolio Prioritization

It can be necessary to re-prioritize your portfolio, so instead of implementing a decision, you cut back on what you already have in the pipeline. Portfolio prioritization gave LINAK a boost .

The management had observed bottlenecks in the project pipeline. It simply progressed too slowly, and adding more resources did not generate more output. Inspired by lean, they took a look at the project list and made the difficult decision to implement a strict order of priority and remove approximately half the projects. Only those projects assessed to have the greatest value would be implemented.

According to R&D Manager Claus H. Sørensen, this was a very tough process, especially when they had to call some of their customers to tell them their product modifications were being put on stand-by. Afterwards, Claus H. Sørensen gathered the remaining project teams together and asked them to revise their schedules to give a more realistic idea of when they would be finished. The only constraints were that they had to work towards completion at the end of a quarter and they had to be finished within a period of three, six or 12 months.

The agreement with the projects also consisted of drawing up a 'LINAK Innovation Treaty', which was signed by LINAK's CEO, Bent Jensen. In the treaty, the management and the employees agreed to follow a set of ground rules. One of the rules was that no one, with the exception of a few specialists, was allowed to work on more than two projects at a time, and project managers were only allowed to work on three projects at a time.

In exchange for these ground rules, everyone agreed to make every effort to comply with the quarterly takt. A number of other initiatives were introduced as well, including a permanent steering committee for every project and fast access to management decisions. Finally, everyone agreed that delays could not be solved simply by extending project periods. In urgent situations, it would be possible to increase staffing on individual projects.

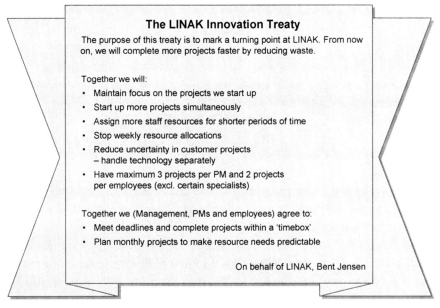

Figure 6.10. The LINAK Innovation Treaty

Another example of portfolio prioritization comes from an American electronics manufacturer. At the beginning of the recession in the 1990s, the company was forced to reduce their R&D costs by 30 percent.

One morning, the CEO convened an early meeting with the project owners of the approx. 300 R&D projects that were in progress at the time. He told them they had to reduce their R&D budgets by 50 percent. After hours of hard work, the team managed to identify 200 projects for cancellation. The CEO then asked which of the 100 remaining projects would benefit the most from receiving extra resources. A total of 30 projects were identified, and their budgets were increased by 100 percent.

The following year, the company launched more products than they had the previous year. They called the method '4-4-2'. No, it is not a soccer formation; it means 'kill 4, keep 4 and double 2'.

Portfolio Overview as a Horserace

A very good approach to simplifying portfolio management can be to introduce various management tools. Traditionally, lean seeks to avoid overly complicated management. For example, if the portfolio can be visualized on the wall, there is no reason to do it on a computer. And if the management can be decentralized and brought close to the employees who use the planning in their work – fantastic. We have an example of a simple management tool from ECCO's prototyping design unit in Thailand.

The prototype department receives hand and computer drawings and material samples from all over the world, which they use to produce the first full-sized prototypes. Sometimes, quite a lot of development work is needed to transform the material received from the creative shoe designer into a shoe that works in practice. There are around 50 to 70 prototypes in progress at a time, distributed among 8 to 16 people. There is a lot of waiting time, because some of the problems that arise have to be solved by the designer, who may be in Italy, the USA or France. It sometimes it can take up to two weeks for the developer to get hold of the designer or for the new material to arrive.

The department management needs to maintain flow in the portfolio in order to be sure that the projects will be completed before the new season. In the past, the head of department maintained an overview of all the projects on a list, which he tried to keep up-to-date. Furthermore, there was no 'owner' of the individual shoes. If a project had problems, the employee would put the shoe aside and start on a new one. When a project was finished, the employee would start a new project, or return to one that had been put aside to finish it.

There were three problems with this approach. The manager did not know where each shoe was in the process, he did not know the status of the overall portfolio, and the employees alternated among many shoes, sometimes with several people working on the same shoe.

A new planning tool was developed in the form of a large whiteboard with 70 lines. A standard phase model for the prototypes was also introduced: upper approved, insole and pattern finished, sole and last finished, mounting and fitting finished etc. This gave the employees responsible for the shoe the freedom

Figure 6.11. Visual Project Portfolio Management

When starting up a new prototype, an employee is appointed owner of the prototype from beginning to end (one responsible person per shoe). A drawing of the shoe is put up on the board along with the employee's initials, and the employee plans a process, taking into account the shoe's complexity and the problems he or she foresees. The process plan is posted on the board, and a day is allocated to each phase in the process. The employee begins working on the shoe and updates the status of the shoe before going home. Status is updated by marking the realized day for each phase with a red or green magnet indicating whether the prototype is on track.

The management team starts each morning in front of an updated portfolio board according to a set agenda and discusses where action is needed to ensure efficient progression in the portfolio.

After finishing each prototype, the number of days it took to pass through the system is written on the board. This promotes a discussion about how the process can be shortened and improved. This discussion also includes evaluation of cooperation with the designers, marketing, production and other external relations.

By implementing the changes described here, ECCO has achieved several things:

- The employees feel a sense of ownership for the individual prototypes and have a stronger sense of responsibility and professional pride.

- The management has a common overview of the work in progress and of any problems.
- The managers come out from behind their desks and become more visible and directly involved in the daily operations.
- Finally, visiting designers, development and marketing people can see the progress of their prototypes.
- Although it looks a bit massive, the board is actually much simpler than the old paper-based system that never was up-to-date.

Most projects in innovation organizations will be much more complicated than in the above case. However, this example of visual management can hopefully inspire others to make similar changes to how they manage their project portfolios.

Measuring Project Focus and Progress

The management needs to be able to monitor the state of the portfolio to determine its progress and whether there are problems with any of the projects. This need for follow-up can result in all kinds of advanced reporting systems. And while they may produce detailed and informative status reports, there is a tendency to spend too much time on reporting and too little on problem-solving.

LINAK found itself in a similar situation, with a management in need of some sort of follow-up that was not immediately available in the projects. It was clear from the outset that the measurement system needed to provide progress information on a weekly basis so that management could react quickly.

Simply registering the employee's time consumption on the individual projects would not give a true picture. The number of hours spent on a task is not a true indication that the project is moving forward. So the management decided to measure progress instead.

Furthermore, they needed to come up with a mechanism to ensure that the projects also benefited from the registration process so it would not be perceived as a waste of time.

They decided on a simple measurement system in which the project managers report two things every week:

- Whether the projects had the resources at their disposal which had been promised them. This, they called project focus.

- And how many milestones the projects reached in the previous week compared to their targets, which they called project progress.

This approach let the managers see which projects were lagging behind, and
it allowed the projects to highlight any incidents within the organization that
slowed them down.

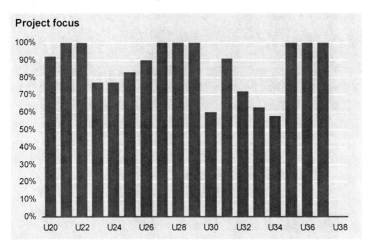

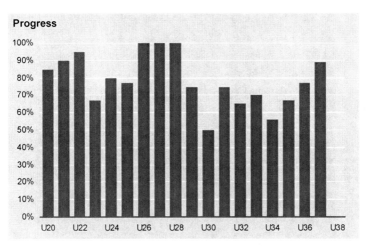

Figure 6.12. Measuring Project Focus and Progress

Management Must Be Able to Navigate in the Project Organization

Many top managers send their project managers and project participants on courses to improve their ability to operate in a project organization. This is, of course, very sensible. However, they often forget dedicating resources to develop their own competencies as well.

If more top managers recognized that managing a project organization requires just as many competencies as managing a line organization, they would be more interested in developing their own competencies.

The top manager needs to play the right role in the portfolio management process. The top managers involved in the process function like an executive board for the projects. You need to carry on a dialog at a certain abstraction level, because the aim is not to solve technical problems. It takes proper training and lots of practice to become good at leading this kind of dialog and to maintain the right level. But you can come a long way towards helping the organization by obtaining an overview and establishing transparency in the process of translating the company's strategy into well-defined projects.

Literature:

Ahrengot, Niels & Niels Søndergaard: "Basic Governance of Projects". Implement A/S, 2007.
Benefield, Gabrielle & Pete Deemer: "The Scrum Primer". Yahoo, 2006.
Cederholm, Eggert & Niels Søndergaard: "Project Governance: Steering Committees That Don't Chicken Out". Implement.
Cooper, Robert G., Scott Edgett & Elko J. Kleinschmidt: *Portfolio Management for New Products*. Basic Books; 2nd edition. January 3, 2002.
Gualati, Ranjay & Nitin Nohria: "Tasting the Fruits of Effective Innovation". Harvard Business School/*Financial Times*, 2009.
Levine, Harvey A.: *Project Portfolio Management*. Wiley & Sons, 2005.
Meyer, Marissa: "Don't Kill Projects; Morph Them". Google Inc. & Stanford University. YouTube, 2009.

Chapter 7
Projects Create Customer Value

Until now, we have limited ourselves to the structures and processes around innovation work. In this chapter, we will take a closer look at projects, which is where knowledge is really transformed into value. They represent a melting pot of needs, ideas, possible solutions, prototypes, competencies, collaboration etc.

Projects are also the moment of truth for the organization. In addition to focusing on finding innovative solutions to customer needs, projects are also where the organization meets the real world. The ideas and competencies of employees, as well as their ability to control innovation processes become visible. They can then be assessed by customers and compared to the competition. The company's ability to succeed with its innovation projects has a direct impact on the bottom line. For example, when talking of fast response to customer needs, even relatively small reductions in project time can have a surprisingly large effect on profits. And, of course, the more important the new solution is, the more this is true.

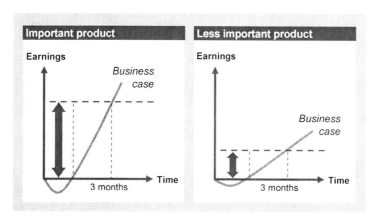

Figure 7.1. Differences in Earnings on Two Different Products with a Three-Month Delay

Development time is a particularly decisive factor that many companies focus on. As previously mentioned 3,000 global senior executives responded that their biggest challenge in innovation was "lengthy development times". The leaders

C. Sehested, H. Sonnenberg, *Lean Innovation*, DOI 10.1007/978-3-642-15895-7_8,
© Springer-Verlag Berlin Heidelberg 2011

surveyed were not satisfied with their companies' ability to quickly transform knowledge into value. The amount of time it takes to get from need to full market launch is a significant factor for ensuring the agility that is increasingly necessary for modern companies. Of course, speed makes no difference if what you make does not create value from the customer's point of view. The tempo of the projects should not be increased at the expense of customer value.

Lean in Projects

Lean in projects is about both 'doing the right thing' and 'doing it right'. Thus, the two primary challenges are:

- How can we guarantee that the outcome of the project meets the intended need?
- How do you develop a fast and efficient process which ensures the above, knowing full well that not everything is known in advance?

The project managers we have spoken to claim the following positive effects from lean: More team members do what they say they will do; higher quality work and lower risk; better coordination and a stronger sense of ownership when it comes to relations both within and outside the project. Overall, better results can be achieved from the innovation process, while reducing resource and time consumption.

Projects Integrate Knowledge Across Disciplines

In highly innovative companies and knowledge-based organizations, the majority of the employees are involved in transforming knowledge into value. This knowledge work is organized as projects. Consequently, projects will be where knowledge workers spend most of their time. Projects are the essence of knowledge creation. The project process is thus the most important process in an innovation-oriented company. It is cross-organizational and aims to integrate relevant knowledge in a solution that can create customer value as quickly as possible. In doing that, the project process must balance the potential solutions with the market objectives.

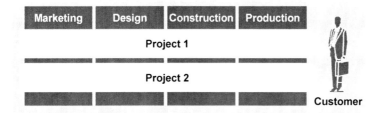

Figure 7.2. Projects Create Customer Value

Conflicts of interest can easily arise between projects and the line organiza-tion. It is therefore important that the executive management both understands and supports the way projects work. This support and understanding is just as important as focus on sales, business development, professional development, financial numbers and budget processes.

More Innovation and Less Operations

Western companies are undergoing a process of change leading to less focus on operations and more on development. This change is, to some extent, the result of more individual and higher consumer demands for products and services. But even more significant is the impact of offshoring production processes to low-wage countries combined with increased automation of the remaining produc-tion. Development, including projects, is increasingly becoming a core aspect of western companies.

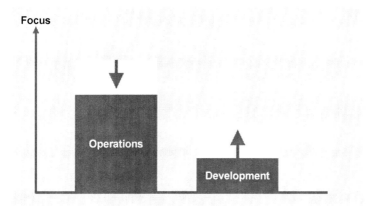

Figure 7.3. The Shift in Companies From Operations to Development

Parallel with this process, we also see new technologies, competencies and types of cross-organizational and cross-industry collaboration creating brand new business opportunities. These business opportunities can only be realized through intelligent and focused project work. Innovation work that has traditionally been a collaboration between departments within a company will increasingly take place as a collaboration between subsidiaries in many different countries and even with external partner firms.

Apple provides an excellent example of this phenomenon. After launching their iPhone in June 2007, a sector analyst bought the phone, not to call Aunt Edna, but to take it apart. He discovered that nothing on the inside was labeled Apple. Balda from Germany supplied the display module, the touch screen was from Epson, while the processor and memory came from Samsung. Even the user interface makes use of partner firms. For example, Google maps is pre-installed when you buy an iPhone. To a large degree, Apple's innovativeness consists of controlling a network of external innovation partners. Apple calls this network their 'eco-system'.

With a view to even more innovation in the future, including innovation in networks, a professional, committed and uniform approach to projects is essential. This makes projects 'synergy drivers' in the company, going far beyond the small word 'project'.

Companies Have Strengthened Their Project Competencies

Companies that understand the increasing importance of projects have focused on boosting project competencies over a longer period. They understand that strategic development projects only have a strategic effect when carried out properly, therefore they have to be articulated about project methods. They choose many different paths in this process, but most usually include working with a project model, a project office organization, a number of project values, decision-making processes and sets of rules. These methods and structures are often supported by project training for the top management, project managers and project participants.

Project Models Generate Structure and a Common Language

The space race in the 1960s saw the first examples of structured project models. NASA was running huge projects with the aim of getting an American to the surface of the moon before the Russians. And to achieve quality in the extensive development projects, NASA introduced something they called a 'Phased Review Process'.

The next milestone project models came in the early 1980s when the Canadian academic Robert Cooper carried out a large number of case studies on product development. His analyzed how the American automotive industry and its suppliers conducted R&D. In short, his work showed that introducing a phase model like the Stage-Gate process illustrated in Figure 7.4 could produce higher quality faster and ensure better budget adherence.

Inspired by Cooper, many companies follow some sort of project model, typically comprising four-five stages with decision points between each stage. At these decisions points, called gates, a steering committee assesses the project's results and plans/budgets for the next stage. If everything is on track, the date for the next gate is set, and the project moves on to the next stage. If the steering committee discovers serious problems, the project is killed or modified before moving on to the next stage.

Figure 7.4. Cooper's Stage-Gate Process

Each stage in the process usually contains descriptions of work steps, roles and responsibilities as well as templates that must be completed. Similarly, the criteria which the project must meet in order to move on to the next stage are also defined. This type of project model strengthens the project process because it defines a set of minimum requirements and gives the company a common language. If a someone says to a new member of the team, "We will be at Gate 3 in a month", the newcomer will immediately have a good idea of the current status of the project. Everyone knows what 'business case' means, and how solid a 'Gate 2 business case' should be. Having a well-defined process for the who, when and how of decision making is also a strength.

Education Improves Individual Competencies

In addition to establishing phase models, companies also spend significant amounts on training project staff. Some focus on project managers. Others go an important step further and train steering committees and project participants as well.

Project managers are given training in both defining projects and ongoing management. The themes of the training program include project planning, management of project teams, stakeholder analysis and risk assessment. They learn to use various document management and QA systems and can create MS Project plans with large numbers of complex dependencies. In more advanced course modules, project participants also learn feedback and coaching techniques. In larger companies, project manager training is often organized through the HR department's course catalog.

This boosts individual motivation for personal development, but also has significant business-related advantages. Basing cross-organizational project work on the same competencies, standards and methods strengthens the ability to execute efficient projects.

Project Managers Lack Focus on Customer Value and Management

Standardized project models and project manager training establish a common point of departure and greater efficiency in the sea of projects carried out by large organizations. But many organizations which have worked with projects for many years also realize that this is not enough. It is a necessary foundation for project work, of course, but it does not, in itself, guarantee innovative and profitable solutions. Project managers tend to forget that project management is also about customer value and leadership, often taking too administrative an approach. They are too focused on rules, forms and documentation and do not succeed in bringing the project models to life in cooperation with the project participants. We would like to touch upon some of the challenges we have experienced within traditional project models and training programs.

Some types of project manager training strongly emphasize linear processes and computer-based project tools. And in some instances, this is justified. But too much focus on IT tools often indicates an underlying assumption that you can sit in a corner office and figure it out. A project manager, or even worse, a planner, sitting at his or her desk drawing up plans on behalf of everyone else on the project team is not the best start. It can lead to errors due to lack of insight or it can lead to the other team members not feeling a sense of ownership for the plan.

Project models often consist of a great many templates that can or must be completed. Project participants often feel that the only reason many of these forms have to be completed is because the 'system' requires it, even though they may be quite irrelevant for the actual work process in the project. And we often see project teams make significant efforts to avoid the official templates or postpone compulsory documentation until the last minute.

Sometimes unsolved problems can move from one stage in the Stage-Gate process to the next because the quality of the project work was not thorough enough. Of course, this should never happen, but it does anyway. It happens if there is too much focus in the process on what each individual discipline group submits before the gate. And it happens if there is not enough time before reaching the gate to integrate and modify the different sub-solutions.

Value Creation of Project Teams Can Differ Significantly

Nearly all innovation in modern organizations takes place in project teams. As a reader of this book, you have probably participated in such projects, working for them or perhaps having daily or overall responsibility for them. Let's look at two extreme situations: Project A and Project B. The two hypothetical teams have the same assignment and the same professional competencies, but are still very different.

Project A:

The team is very enthusiastic about the project and wants to show the world that their solution is nothing short of genius. They all see the same clear objective and they all feel a deep personal commitment to that objective. They are genuinely interested in the users' situation and problems. They want to help. They feel they make their company even better with the solution they are developing. They inspire each other and are open to ideas and suggestions. They have a common, well-defined approach to how they cooperate which promotes progress and a good overview. They have the right level of competencies individually and the right combination of competencies as a team. They feel a shared sense of responsibility for the project and have fun working together.

Project B:

The overall objective is a bit unclear. Some of the team members do not have a lot of time to work on the project or they prioritize other things higher. To compensate for the low individual participation, the project team is relatively large – 14 members. They feel the project is more of a duty than something that is really important. There are often disputes among the participants from the different departments. People are preoccupied with 'winning' and they consider the priorities of their own department most important. The team also experiences many delays, because all deliverables have to be approved by individual department managers. Throughout the process, different members of the top management make different demands. The participants do not feel there is time to talk to the users. This delays the process. The team always meets in different rooms at different times, and rarely does every team member attend the meetings, because they are unstructured and planned too late.

If the aim of a project is to create something new − which, of course, is the prime objective of an innovation project – then there are significant differences between the business results created by the two teams. The solution developed by project A will undoubtedly be much better than project B's solution. It may even be infinitely better. In an innovative knowledge-based organization, the management team is responsible for establishing a culture and associated processes that result in lots of A-teams.

Roles and Responsibilities Must Be Well-Defined

Several aspects help make an A-team. One of the most important prerequisites is that there is a clear difference between what is and what is not a project. In other words: The distribution of roles and responsibilities between the line organization and the projects must be very well-defined. If this is not the case, it will be difficult to make decisions, practice leadership and promote the right motivation in the project teams. A project-oriented organization requires strong project management capabilities.

The project management must be able to assume responsibility for the company's most important processes – the projects. In many organizations, project management has a lower status than line management. Consequently, the position as project manager tends to be considered temporary, at worst, rendering it impossible to attract talented leaders. The project manager is responsible for the successful completion of the project. He or she functions as a kind of managing director for the individual project. To do this, the manager needs to have the freedom and resources to make the necessary decisions. It is difficult to feel a sense of responsibility for the success of a project and to create an A-team, if others keep interfering, either directly or indirectly. Every time it happens, the rug gets pulled out from under the project manager, and ultimately it becomes impossible for him or her to lead the team. The line management should respect the project manager's responsibilities and only get involved in the project through its steering committee.

A line manager is responsible for motivating and developing the organization's resources and professional discipline competencies. The line manager is also responsible for spotting talent and getting them onboard to help ensure that the organization's competency profile can support the strategy and the projects that realize the strategy.

A steering committee consists of the people who requested the project result or a given solution. Often, the main suppliers of project resources are also represented on the steering committee.

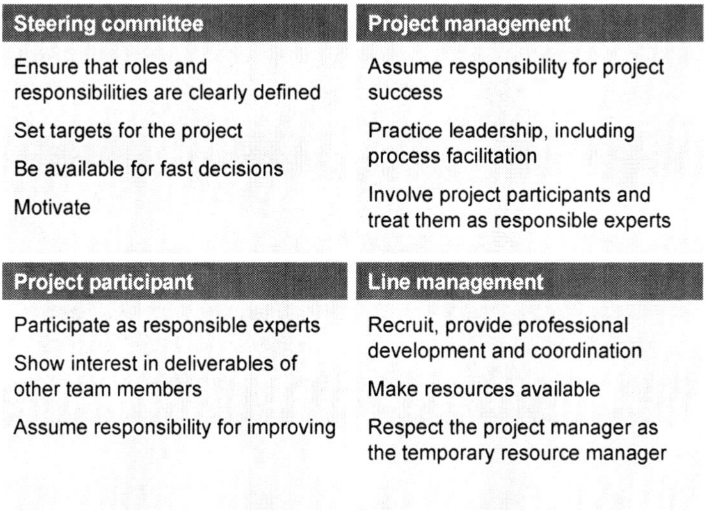

Steering committee	Project management
Ensure that roles and responsibilities are clearly defined	Assume responsibility for project success
Set targets for the project	Practice leadership, including process facilitation
Be available for fast decisions	
Motivate	Involve project participants and treat them as responsible experts

Project participant	Line management
Participate as responsible experts	Recruit, provide professional development and coordination
Show interest in deliverables of other team members	Make resources available
Assume responsibility for improving	Respect the project manager as the temporary resource manager

Figure 7.5. Roles and Responsibilities in a Project Organization

The project team members act as technical experts who can work independently on the projects.

The employees are expected to show an interest in the other members of the team and to promote the crucial integration of the various participating disciplines.

The Value Stream in Innovation

In the innovation process, knowledge is transformed into value. In lean, 'value stream mapping' means following the product or solution throughout the process to see the value that is added along the way. The project process is a value stream that moves from need to solution. It is a unique value stream that is planned individually for each project. It is unique because innovation, by definition, involves solving tasks that have never been solved before. In order for the project value stream to generate maximum value, and to do so as quickly as possible, the project organization must be good at:

- Identifying customer value
- Developing the value stream
- Driving the value stream

Identifying customer value

In a lean culture, the individual project starts with defining the solution that generates the most customer value. This includes both clarifying the customer need and establishing the acceptable solution space. Doing this successfully can minimize one of the biggest sources of innovation waste, i.e. creating solutions that customers don't need. You also avoid over or underdeveloping the solution. Having an interest in and a good understanding of the customers' reality is a collective competency that will make the job easier.

Both mentally and physically, lean project teams are good at 'going to gemba', and learning from the user's reality. In a lean organization, top management and projects teams have a well defined process for working together to establish the right ambitions for innovation projects. They have a close dialog and a common language which establish a vision and a project basis that is both motivational, focused and well-thought-out.

Developing the Value Stream

In practice, building a value stream in a project means to draw up the project's main plan. The purpose of this plan is to produce maximum learning and speed. Thus, the plan needs to be front loaded so the project team can learn as much as possible as quickly as possible. One way to front load and accelerate learning is to make project planning a team effort. Inviting project participants with relevant professional qualifications to participate in the planning process improves the quality of the plan significantly. At the same time, the joint planning process creates a sense of ownership that ensures more communication and drive in the process. Lean project participants are enthusiastic about the project vision and work well together across disciplines. They are interested in what other members of the team are doing and create a 'truly' integrated development team.

The planned value stream works better if the team, during the planning phase, establishes an overview of all the questions associated with the objective of the project and the desired customer value. There may be several hundred questions that together help make the value stream more robust. The value stream is a learning process. Therefore, we must consciously make room for team learning. This requires planning integrated solution models, prototypes, customer contact and tests so they take place at a high frequency. It also requires adequate room/ time for the team to apply the learning obtained from prototyping and tests.

Driving the Value Stream

Driving the value stream suggests an active management role where you do not just blindly follow the process. This active management is strengthened by an environment and physical surroundings that enable visual and engaging collaboration. Managing the value stream means working together to maintain a conscious learning process with a high takt. The team breaks the big questions and the larger deliverables into smaller operational milestones that only span a few weeks. This makes the project more specific and accessible. This breakdown is a prerequisite for achieving a fast learning loop. It also makes coordination among the project's different focus areas easier.

In a lean project a project rhythm needs to be set that everyone agrees on. It can be a weekly project meeting, as an integration point where everyone follows up on individual milestones completed that week. This is how the milestones create 'pull' and flow in the value stream. A lean project team collaborates actively on the plan. This work is operationalized efficiently with the help of a visual project board. An essential element in the planning process is that the team follows up on progress more than on resource consumption. That is why there should be weekly focus on what you have learned, the questions you have answered and what milestones you have achieved.

Examples of Lean in Projects

The key to successful lean innovation is not only 'what you do', but, more importantly, 'how you do what you do'.

We would like to present three examples that we feel both operationalize and illustrate the lean principles very well. They can help project managers and team establish joint responsibility, bring focus to their projects, promote progress and generate results. Many project teams have asked themselves how their working methods could be improved and then experimented with various approaches. The outcome is these methods. We want to emphasize that the methods are not an exhaustive list of how to implement lean in project work. There are many other methods out there as well. But the following methods work in practice and they help incorporate leadership into the projects:

- The visual project board
- Front loading in projects
- Continuous improvements with project forums

The Visual Project Board

The visual project board is a board or poster displaying all necessary information for defining the project and following-up on the project. It is a kind of extra-large, interactive 'one-pager' on the project. The idea is that you can see the status of the project on the board, and can plan, follow-up and adjust the project in a simple way using Post-its and markers. The board is so simple, in fact, that some project managers initially find it childish or ridiculous. But once they get over their professional pride, project participants discover that the board has a positive effect on the project work.

The basic objective of the board is to increase focus within the individual project. This can be achieved in many ways, for instance, in the project definition process or in the way team members communicate with each other. Many companies choose to increase focus by having the team members work together in the same location or room. A virtual project room can also be used, but face-to-face is much preferable.

In Munich, the BMW team gathers together physically at their research and innovation center (*Forschung und Innovations Zentrum* - FIZ), when they begin developing a new car model. And when IDEO in San Francisco develops solutions for their customers, it takes place in a project room where you can draw on every wall and where their innovation principles and visions are visible to everyone in the room. In Toyota's development projects, they have the *oobeya*, the big room where the walls display every important element of the project – objectives, progress, risks etc.

The visual board, the 1 x 2 meter board or the poster is 'the big room'. The visual project board is the connecting thread in results-oriented, attentive and engaging project work. It helps the project manager to lead and helps the project team to see the big picture, assume responsibility and participate. The board is a very simple standard that can be used as the project manager's agenda for kick-off, planning and continuous follow-up on the project. And since this standard is very intuitive and uncomplicated, it is easy for the entire team to work together efficiently.

But what do you do if you have 100 projects in progress? Do you have to have 100 boards hung up all over the place? Ramboll Oil & Gas does not have exactly 100 projects in progress concurrently, but they still have quite a lot. And since they do not have room for boards for every project, they decided to use large posters instead. But even though they are more flexible than boards, they still take up space. So the smaller projects with only one or two participants simply make smaller prints of their posters. Alternatively, several smaller projects can be grouped together on one board or poster.

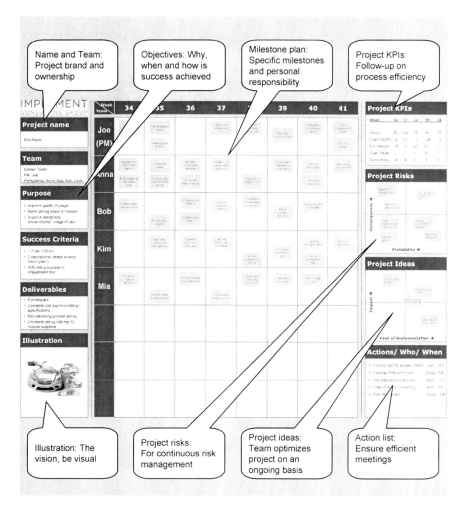

Figure 7.6. Visual Project Board

The board supports two important elements of project management, namely project definition and continuous follow-up. Key activities in defining the project:

- Defining project objectives
- Planning the project
- Establishing Key Performance Indicators (KPIs) for the project
- Mapping project risks
- Holding status meetings
- Replanning of the project

Defining Project Objectives

Determining objectives of a project normally starts with the top management, possibly through a steering committee, requesting a solution to a business challenge in the market. Maybe, the company is losing ground in a market segment or is looking for a way to win customers back again. Such requests are rarely in the form of a specific shopping list you can bring to the store. The request is also rarely in the form of an actual project description. Perhaps it has been a while since the top management were project managers themselves, or maybe the top management is just expressing its wishes in more general and visionary terms than developers and project staff are used to.

In any case, the project team needs to take the management request and reformulate it into something suitable for project work. The team needs to work with the objectives and make them their own. Then they can discuss it with management and get it re-confirmed.

Some project teams are afraid to go back to management for confirmation. They do not want anyone to think they have not understood the assignment. They want to show their ability to take immediate action, they doubt whether the management team has time to talk to them, and they are generally not good at communicating with management, so they just start up the project. That should never happen. The project manager is responsible for ensuring that the team and management have a common and precise understanding of the project objectives. The management team must ensure that the project manager assumes that responsibility and acts accordingly.

Management and project team need to agree on the answers to three questions: Why have we started this project? How will we know if it is a success? What must the project deliver? In other words, there are three important elements in formulating project objectives:

- Purpose: Why have we started the project?
- Success criteria: How do we assess whether it is a success?
- Project deliverables: What should the project deliver when it is finished?

Both purpose and success criteria are closely linked to the potential utility value of the solution for the future users. It is therefore also important early in the project to have a very good understanding of and dialog with the people for whom the solution is should create value. Formulating the objectives defines the ambition level of the solution. Which functionalities in the solution are a must, and which are just nice to have? There are many ways to define functionality, requirements, value proposition etc. We will not go into detail on such methods here, but would like to encourage project teams to try spending more time on objectives than they usually do. This is a type of front loading. When success-ful, it results in higher user value, less 'overengineering', which as we know is waste, fewer costs and happier customers.

There is an interdependence between the purpose, success criteria and deliv-erables. And it is important to define the purpose and success criteria before defining the project deliverables. Many project teams, especially those that are highly specialized, have a tendency to start defining the deliverables too soon, because that is what they find most interesting. Here, management needs to insist on seeing the project's purpose and success criteria.

At the ventilation manufacturer Exhausto, introducing lean innovation has made everyone more conscious and articulate about how quality goals for new products are defined. That is, defining success criteria for the desired product performance. They have implemented continuous measuring points, both in the project process and after market launch. This focus on success criteria and follow-up has resulted in a significant drop in complaints-related costs.

When ECCO starts developing a new shoe, the project team holds a kick-off workshop where a key element is reviewing and discussing the project objec-tives. The objectives originated with the management team, which 'ordered' the new shoe. But the team spends a lot of time discussing it and trying to under-stand it fully. Who is the target group? Why? What current shoe models would be affected by the new model? How many pairs of shoes need to be sold in year 1 before the solution can be called a success? And how does the new model sup-port ECCO's overall objectives and branding strategy?

Should a project team really spend time discussing these things? Or should they assume that this is something management has under control, and just get to work? If you want an A-team rather than a B-team, then time should be devoted to discussing these issues.

Ramboll Oil & Gas had two very different types of customers. One customer type typically starts a project with an open problem, and the first part of the proj-ect focuses on working with the customer to define the objective. The second type of customer defines the problem in detail before contacting Ramboll. They have neither the need nor the patience to discuss it further, and want Ramboll to deliver as specified.

Which of the two customers receives the most value? Which customer is best? As a supplier, you need to know your visiting hours and, of course, to rec-ognize that the person with the need probably understands it better than others. But in the long term, and especially within innovation, you have to stop up and question the objectives, challenge them and make them your own. Doing this will help you stay one step ahead of the competition in the innovation race. It will also make the work process more varied and interesting.

All organizations have both managers and project team members who are neither interested in nor have the time for this discussion. And sometimes people are afraid they will end up in an open discussion club with all talk and no progress or focus. But this particular discussion, when managed properly, can actually provide a clear focus and direction for the project. It minimizes waste and makes the product and the process lean.

Planning the Project

Management needs to have a general understanding of how a lean innovation team efficiently build and work with the project plan. This understanding and interest is necessary, because visual planning involves a different dialog between the steering committee and the project team than most managers are used to. In lean innovation, the plan is something the team works with actively. It is a team-based tool and, to a lesser extent, a form of documentation to satisfy the management team, the project office or controllers from the finance department.

Figure 7.7. Visual Planning

A project team will typically receive a draft of a main plan at the start of a project. Without this draft plan, it would not be possible to dimension the project. After defining clear objectives for the project, the team should design the unique value stream (= main plan), that they are willing to stand behind. And if at this point they already see problems with meeting important milestones, the issues should be discussed with the steering committee as soon as possible. The main plan should be a milestone plan, not an activity plan. This is because it is more important in innovation projects to manage delivery quality and time-to-market than resource consumption.

To turn the main plan into a useful tool, the team transforms the first part into a visual plan only spanning 6 to 8 weeks. The visual plan is usually some sort of table on a poster or board. Along the x-axis is the time dimension, with one box for each week. Down the y-axis there is space for the project participants, usually a core team of 4 to 6 people representing the required specialist disciplines. Using Post-its, the project participants post their individual milestones in the weeks where they aim to have them completed.

There should never be three-four weeks without milestones. If the first large milestone is in four weeks, it needs to be broken down into smaller milestones or partial results to be achieved every week. After posting all the milestones, each participant consults the team members from whom they need input before they can achieve their own milestones on time.

Visual planning has many advantages. Everyone involved in the project feels a sense of ownership of the plan because they have made it themselves. Everyone can see the big picture and understands that milestones must be achieved on time. They have actually looked directly at the colleague who needs the deliverable in order to do their job and promised completion on a given date. Working with a visual plan improves leadership because not everything needs to pass the project manager's desk. This saves the project manager from the uncomfortable task of dictating when various project participants have to finish their deliverables. They have to be finished exactly when other members of the team need that output in a high enough quality to be able to complete their own deliverables on time. The work with the visual plan presumes that the team comprises technical experts who are capable of assuming responsibility. The project manager's role is to control the process, not the content. Almost as a matter of course, a visual plan sets a faster pace for the project work by making it both specific and 'urgent' at the same time.

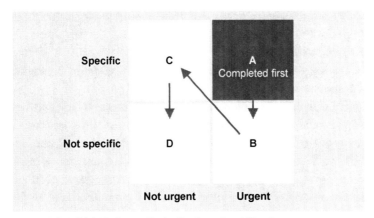

Figure 7.8. Which Tasks are Typically Completed First?

There is a tendency for project team members, and people in general, to start working on whatever is most urgent. And if there are a lot of tasks that seem equally urgent, they start with whatever is most well-specified. The visual plan's weekly takt helps create a 'positive urgency', and the break-down into well-defined milestones makes the work specific.

Visual planning is a central element in lean. A visual plan is hands-on, with many milestones and a takt – typically a weekly takt – making it possible to follow the progress and enabling team learning on a weekly basis. Within IT development, work methods with an even faster takt are used. Under the concept of Agile Development, we have the Scrum project framework, which consists of a daily follow-up takt and planning windows called 'Sprints' that are sometimes only one or two weeks long.[2] That serves the same purpose as visual planning in lean, i.e. to generate focus and fast learning through a high takt and to promote cooperation and ownership of the plan.

If you are on a steering committee for a project that utilizes visual planning, you will have to get used to a new type of dialog with the project team. The visual plan is not documented in an IT system or PowerPoint. It can only be found in one place – on the wall of the project room. And to obtain a status update, you will have to do as Toyota's Taiichi Ohno does when he "goes to gemba"; you will have to go the place where the project is being carried out. As a manager, you need to bear in mind that asking for status reports to obtain information starts a process that occupies resources from

---

[2] Agile Development is a blanket term for software development methods that emphasize regular delivery of value to the customer through iterative development. Scrum is an example of an agile project method.

the projects. And you need to ask yourself whether the knowledge obtained from reading a status report really makes you more informed. Everyone who works on projects knows full-well the energy that goes into making such reports.

When you start using visual planning, you may find some project managers less than enthusiastic. At least in the beginning. How can a plan using Post-its be better than a detailed MS Project plan that shows all the dependencies, critical paths, the total resource consumption and many other KPIs? Some have even asked what happens if someone switches the Post-its. To this we can only emphasize that ownership, teamwork and fast learning are more important than full control of every little detail. After testing the process for a few weeks, even the most stubborn project managers realize that visual planning is actually not a soft, kindergarten technique. It is a hard, consequent and concrete method, because everything is out in the open. There is no place to hide for anyone who does not share the objectives and does not make an effort for the team.

At the Ramboll Oil & Gas offices in Denmark, almost every project utilizes visual planning. They introduced visual planning through pilot projects and case-oriented team training. And the nearly 200 people who use the method today agree that joint ownership and the improved coordination have reduced the amount of rework in the projects.

Claus H. Sørensen, who initiated LINAK's lean innovation program, also has positive experiences with visual planning. Introducing it required a great deal of perseverance because it changed the fundamental working methods throughout the organization. At the time this book was written, LINAK was in its fourth year of utilizing visual planning in its innovation projects. "It has enabled us to generate more ownership and visibility, as well as getting the MS Project plans out of the project manager's computer," he says.

Establishing Key Performance Indicators for the Project

The point of Key Performance Indicators (KPIs) is to establish a foundations for fact-based follow-up. In lean, follow-up is a central aspect of creating continuous improvements. KPIs are nothing new in the business world. In fact, there is almost too much focus on them. Or rather, there is too much focus on how to establish advanced KPIs, and too little on how to use them in a way that increases result focus among people carrying out the projects.

In the world of lean, follow-up is based on the premise that the people doing the work are not stupid and that they are also interested in knowing how well they do their job. In the world of lean, the project team has full responsibility for the success of the project. Consequently, the project team members are the ones who discuss what characterizes an efficient project process and who agree on the aspects of the project requiring follow-up. Some project KPIs which could be useful:

- Product target cost
- Resource consumption
- Project intensity (hours/participants)
- Completion level of tests
- Number of milestones reached per week
- Number of times users have given feedback
- Team temperature

The KPIs should be so easy to obtain that the project team can do it themselves, either by printing reports from existing systems or by asking around in the project team. When the project is under way, the KPIs are written on the board with a marker at every follow-up meeting.

Mapping Project Risks

Being proactive and addressing potential threats to the project's success at an early stage is a necessary part of all project work. Risk management is another way to front load a project. That is, it is a good way to accelerate the level of critical knowledge in the early phase of the project.

But what can lean do for risk management? Make it a team process. Lean ensures that team members spend more time working together to identify risks, understand them and act accordingly than to document and calculate them. And by project risks, we mean the things that can threaten the project process. When looking at the product there is often a need for more comprehensive technical risk analysis, such as FMEA, health and safety assessments etc.

After the joint project plan has been developed, the risk mapping starts. The team discusses all potential threats to the project objective. And, here, they should think in broad terms within technology, internal policy, sales processes, market conditions, competitors etc. Brainstorming is a good way to identify risks, and afterwards, the risks can be placed in order of priority in a matrix on the board. The most serious risks lead to new milestones in the visual plan, while the less serious risks lead to preventive or mitigating actions on the action list.

All projects involve risks. This is because a project is by definition some-thing you are doing for the first time. That is why a responsible project team is always aware of the obstacles that arise and they make sure to act on them.

Conducting Status Meetings

The board is very useful for establishing the project foundation. But the main purpose of the board is to turn the plan into something the team works with on an ongoing basis. The structure of the board therefore serves to facilitate a con-tinuous follow-up process in the project team. And continuous follow-up is key to strengthening the project's internal learning loop. Learning and knowledge should be shared as often as possible among the project participants, and the best structure for promoting this is regular project meetings.

It is better to have short project meetings frequently than to have long proj-ect meetings less frequently. However, the best way to plan project meetings naturally depends on they type of project. The vast majority of projects will benefit from a weekly 30-minute project meeting. And it is actually possible to create value in just half an hour. In the beginning, it will be difficult, but after a few weeks, everyone will have caught on. The different areas on the board work well as agenda items for the follow-up meeting.

Weekly project meeting (30 min.) – Agenda

1. Follow up on actions from last meeting
2. Follow up on completed milestones and upcoming milestones
3. Follow up on KPIs
4. Risk assessment and improvement ideas
5. Conclude and define actions

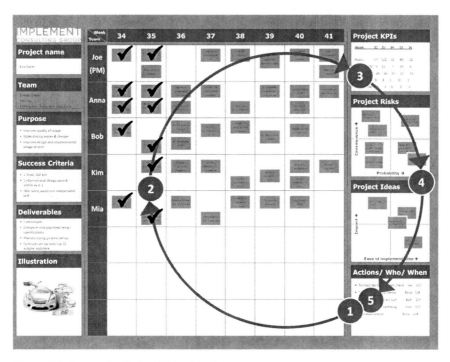

Figure 7.9. Process for Project Status Meetings

The meeting is then adjourned and documented. There is no need to write separate meeting minutes. A participant does not have to remember every decision made at the meeting in order to write imprecise and subjective minutes which the recipients might not see until three days later. All the vital output from the meeting is noted on the board. Board-based follow-up meetings are the essence of lean project management.

At Ramboll Oil & Gas, some of the projects are actually able to keep follow-up meetings down to just 20 minutes. This creates value for the project participants, because in the past they could easily sit alone at their desks for three weeks without really knowing what was going on in the project. With weekly meetings, the project manager emphasizes the importance of the project.

In order for the follow-up meetings to work and be efficient, it is necessary separate the process and the content. The process is what you follow up on at the weekly meeting. And when the discussion turns too technical it must be handled in a professional manner. If the meeting takes too long because two of the five participants had an important technical discussion, this can have a negative impact on the motivation of the other participants. And that must never happen. If technical discussions are necessary, everyone needs to agree to extend the meeting by the amount of time needed to complete the discussion. Alternatively, a separate problem-solving meeting can be booked with the participation of only the relevant specialists.

We have seen many teams with an ambition to meet weekly that they could not achieve. At the end of every follow-up meeting, they tried to find a date for the next meeting that fit everyone's schedules. That was almost never possible within a week's time. And even when they did manage to book meetings, they would take place at different times on different days week after week. This caused a quite a bit of uncertainty and many misunderstandings with regard to meeting participation and milestone achievements. To make the project follow-up an efficient process, we recommend holding the meetings on the same day every week in addition to keeping them short and frequent. The project manager can, for example, hold follow-up meetings every Tuesday from 9.00 to 9.30 am, which allows him to book all weekly meetings for the 2 or 3 months in one go. This establishes a takt that everyone recognizes and the project participants quickly integrate them into their routines.

Replanning

The project reaches the end of the visual planning window about every 6 to 8 weeks. The next 8 weeks of the project needs to be planned at an operational level. In some types of projects, it will necessary to replan more often, for example certain IT projects or projects that move into unknown territory. If you operate with a 6 week takt, a replanning workshop of approximately 2-3 hours is sufficient.

The planning part, itself, is carried out in the same way as when the project was planned the first time around, using Post-its as milestones.

And since the project team is gathered together anyway to work on planning, the workshop is also a perfect opportunity to reassess project objectives, i.e. purpose, success criteria and deliverables. Is the project still on track or are new initiatives needed to ensure the desired quality and effect?

This is also a good time to do a risk assessment that is more thorough than what takes place at the weekly follow-up meetings.

Visual Management Helps the Project Manager, but It Takes Practice

Regular routines around the project boards help promote concretization, visibility and joint responsibility. For the project manager, the routines and the structure can help strengthen his or her role as leader. The structure can be one of the fix-points in the role as leader, and will probably help the inexperienced project managers more than the experienced. However, this structure creates value for the experienced project manager, as well, because it helps less-experienced team members to see their own role and the direction more clearly.

The regular routines can also help generate more creative solutions. Initially, it might sound like process and structure could make the work less impulsive and thus less creative. But as long as the structure isn't only structure for the sake of structure – which it is not in lean – then creativity will be promoted in at least three ways:

1. It will save time on documentation and reporting. The time you save can be spent on creative value generation.
2. Many people are actually more creative when they have some kind of framework or direction. For instance, it is not very easy to look at a blank piece of paper and just come up with a good idea for a new product.
3. A 'forced' team process ensures that the team meets frequently. And because a team is often more creative than an individual, there will be more opportunities for creative idea generation.

An efficient visual process is primarily the project manager's responsibility, and for most project managers, it will require some practice, perseverance and patience in the beginning. Many project managers, like other leaders, have a history as specialists. Lean project management requires leadership and facilitation competencies. You have to be able to lead a planning workshop around the board, and know what to do if, say, a participant appears indifferent, formulates imprecise milestones etc. You have to be able to steer the discussion and ensure focus on results at the project meetings, and everyone has to make contributions and assume responsibility. Project managers who are able to maintain the visual process will, after five to eight lean project meetings, discover that they are much better at their jobs.

Management Has a Responsibility for Making the Visual Process Work

It is management that initiates the work with project boards, so naturally management needs to motivate the knowledge workers that use them. This is best done by showing an interest in the work. It has a positive effect when managers ask about the work and respects the project manager's efforts to get the visual board up and running. Management should also ask questions if the milestones have not been checked off and make it known that they expect perseverance in following the methods. The management team can support the project managers with facilitation training and help start-up and implement board-based follow-up meetings. They need to understand that facilitating a visual project process is not the easiest thing in the world to do if you are not used to it.

Management should support a lean project culture where there is room to work visually and where the project participants have the opportunity to generate maximum focus on the assignment. This is best achieved when the project team sits together. However it is not always possible for all projects to sit together physically. Some projects are carried out across regions, and others are simply too small for it to make sense. I these cases, virtual web-based methods can be used for the continuous follow-up.

The management team can support the establishment of fora where knowledge is shared among people working with visual project management. Such knowledge-sharing events will help speed up the process of establishing a lean culture. The good process ideas will be shared and improved, while everything that does not work automatically will be dropped or forgotten.

Front Loading in Projects

We have mentioned the concept of front loading in several contexts. The purpose of front loading is to accelerate learning, especially at project start-up, where there is a risk of making important decisions based on too little knowledge. This calls for increased resource consumption at the start of the project. If you do a good job front loading, you will find that you create better solutions for the customers. And you will find that the projects are completed faster. This concept is also illustrated in Allen Ward's study: "The Second Toyota Paradox – How Delaying Decisions Can Make Better Cars Faster".

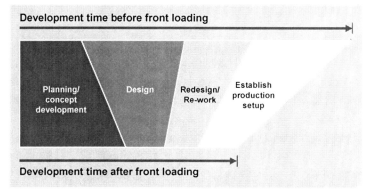

Figure 7.10. The Effect of Good Front Loading

Inadequate front loading may even make things worse. And it is not always easy to determine when you have enough knowledge to proceed with the project. It takes steady nerves. When everyone is standing around you and wants to proceed with your output, it is hard to say, "Wait! – we need to come up with one more alternative solution or do two more customer interviews". One thing is certain, front loading takes nerves of steel and the ability to stand up to external pressures. But the team and the organization also need to have a common understanding of the what front loading is, and there have to be structured methods that can be brought into play. We have often heard people call all kinds of discussions in projects front loading, because that somehow made it more acceptable for everything to take a little longer. That is, of course, not how it should be. And it is natural for the person responsible for resources to be a bit concerned about using more resources at the start of the project. That is often where the projects seem a little 'loose', so managers wonder "Is that really where more money needs to be allocated".

We would like to show two examples of practical methods that can make front loading more structured and predictable:

- Front loading with 200 questions
- Front loading with customer involvement

Front loading with 200 Questions

The 200 questions method is one way to front load. It is good for innovation because it addresses the core of innovation, namely gathering knowledge as quickly and efficiently as possible.

The approach is simple. The project team brainstorms the questions that they need answered at that particular time in order to create the best possible solution. The questions should be varied and should deal with customers, markets, guarantees, service, production conditions, cost price etc. The team then prioritizes the questions according to the resources and the time that is available. Some questions may not be answered right away, others might be answered through qualified guessing.

The project team discusses which methods are needed to answer the remaining questions, for example analysis of complaints, user observation, gathering information from colleagues, competition studies etc. The questions are then distributed among the team members and everyone goes out to find all the answers they can. Finally, the answers are shared with the rest of the team one to two weeks later.

It is a good idea to brainstorm immediately after defining the project. Reviewing the project's purpose and success criteria, as well as any deliverables, milestone plans, KPIs and risks at the start of the 200-question workshop provides a good and relevant basis for generating the questions. It is important that the team works together to formulate the questions. It is interesting for all participants to hear what kinds of questions team members from other disciplines ask. And it is just as relevant for everyone on the team to also be interested in all 200 answers. If this interest is not there, you lose a chance to create a high-performance team that shares the same vision and sticks together through thick and thin.

LINAK once conducted a 200-question workshop without the participation of the quality assurance department. At an advanced stage of the project, problems developed because this dimension in the knowledge collection had not been sufficiently covered. The learning from LINAK is that you should not be afraid of inviting too many to the brainstorming session.

On another occasion, LINAK's use of the method generated surprisingly great value. At an early front loading workshop, the participants from production asked what demands an American production line had to live up to. Some were surprised to learn that production had plans to manufacture the product in the US. It was not part of the project description and had not been mentioned in any other context. This example shows how important it is to share questions and answers with the entire project team. You can generate a lot of value by inviting people to front loading sessions who would not normally be involved in the 'real' project until much later in the process. It gives the team a better opportunity to address key changes at an early stage, thus avoiding expensive delays at the end of the project.

Front Loading with Customer Involvement

It is crucial that the project begins as quickly as possible to gather knowledge about the needs it has to meet and about how a potential solution should look. There are many ways to obtain this knowledge – from observing the usage situation to allowing customers to test physical prototypes. One approach we would like to describe in more detail here is called 'Panel of Experts'.

This method is built up like a customer focus group. It is called 'Panel of Experts' because the customers are considered experts in their own situation, just like the project's participants are each experts in their own particular fields. 'Panel of Experts' is thus a meeting between experts. But this kind of workshop is interesting because it collects different types of information for use in the analysis while at the same time enabling the testing of early solutions.

Figure 7.11. Customer Involvement with 'Panel of Experts'

The workshop is prepared by the project team, which asks the questions they want the customers to answer. Because some questions are best asked in a questionnaire, the customer workshop generally begins with the participants completing a questionnaire. But, there are also questions that cannot be answered in a questionnaire. So the customers are divided into three smaller groups which take turns completing three other types of assignments. One assignment asks the participants to describe their usage situation. The second asks the participants to build or describe a desired solution, possibly with the help of solution modules. In the third task, the group comments on a series of potential alternative solutions the project team has developed in advance. The solutions may be in any form, from drawings on a piece of paper to actual prototypes. Finally, the participants are asked to brainstorm on future trends.

After the workshop, the project team can return to the original questions and draw conclusions from the responses.

The individual methods that comprise the workshop can be adjusted as needed, but the overall structure of the workshop makes for an efficiently information collection process. This is because a variety of question types can be used, including open and closed questions, analytical questions and questions about the solutions. Even though the workshop takes place at an early stage in the project, it is important that the team is also able to show potential solutions to the customers. It forces the team to begin the process of formulating solutions and gives them a good understanding of the customers' wishes and needs at a very early stage in the process.

Continuous Improvements with Project Forums

In the individual project, continuous improvement is a natural and integral element. But it is also important to work on a general level with how to continuously improve the organization's project competencies. Again, LINAK has a good example of a practical way to initiate this process. They gathered the project managers together every other week for a two-hour session they called a project manager forum.

The project manager forum started with a workshop to identify waste in the form of problems that prevented projects from progressing efficiently. The list of waste was very long. Subsequent meetings took place regularly every other week, with one or two items from the list making up the topic of each meeting. Two project managers were assigned to each problem, and they had two weeks to investigate the problem and find a solution. This preliminary work was presented at the project manager forum, and the solution had to be implemented by the following meeting. This steady frequency became the process for every single improvement idea, ensuring continuous development and optimization of project conditions and removing each obstacle one at a time. Because the process was primarily driven by the project managers, the solutions could also be implemented quickly.

Project Work Can Reach New Heights with Lean

Project staff are an important resource for a company, because they are the ones who actually develop the solutions that are needed to realize the company's strategy. Thus, it is of strategic importance that top management focuses on how projects progress and also understands how to organize and motivate the project organization.

Projects represent a huge potential for creating a successful lean culture. The effect of well-defined project solutions delivered fast and on time is undisputable. The company can tap into an enormous potential and open new market opportunities if, in addition to formulating winning strategies, they also have the agility to realize them.

Lean can be the solution. Most leaders of innovation processes should appreciate the idea of establishing routines for continuous improvements. Imagine if your employees are so motivated to get involved that they assume a whole new level of responsibility for the process and for its continuous improvement. The company is practically guaranteed better results. However, companies can also benefit from 'just' getting continuous improvement loops implemented. It can start a powerful positive spiral in which the employees, through improvements, actually increase their motivation, make more improvements and are more satisfied at work. Having employees who both work better and are truly enthusiastic about their work represents an almost infinite potential for most companies.

Literature:

Cooper, Robert G.: *Winning at New Products*. Addison-Wesley, 1993.

Cooper, Robert G.: "Third-Generation New Product Processes". *Journal of Product Innovation Management*, no. 11, 1994.

Cooper, Robert G.: "Stage-Gate Innovation Process". www.provenmodels.com.

Radeka, Katherine: "Visual Project Boards". Whittier Consulting Group Inc. 2006.

Sviokla, John: "In Praise of Ecosystems". DiamondCluster International Inc. 2007.

Ward, Allen, John J. Christiano, Jeffrey K. Liker & Durward K. Sobek: "The Second Toyota Paradox: How Delaying Decisions Can Make Better Cars Faster". *Sloan Management Review*, 1995.

Ward, Allen, Jeffrey K. Liker, Durward K. Sobek: "Toyota's Principle of Set-Based Concurrent Engineering". *MIT Sloan Management Review*, 1999.

www.labs.google.com.

Chapter 8
The Role of Project Support in Innovation

The ambition to make innovation processes a competitive asset also involves the functions that provide project support. For example, ECCO has a lab in the line function that tests the shoes' grip, durability and comfort for the development projects.

In many innovation projects, most of the development work actually takes place outside the projects. Sometimes project support is not even part of the company, but is provided by external suppliers. Take another example from ECCO, which does not develop its own last for its shoe prototypes. Instead, they are developed by a subsupplier in another country. Other examples of project support include, purchasing, quality, documentation of drawings, patent analysis, prototypes, market communication and developing sales material. This chapter will concentrate on the support functions associated with project work – project support.

Some support tasks are purely operational, because they provide a standard service for the project. Others are development tasks, such as designing and constructing new packaging. In these types of tasks, the work of the support functions is commissioned by the projects. Thus, the projects are the customers and the support functions are the suppliers.

Project support	Administrative support
Lab	HR/recruitment
Prototype workshop	Finance
Market survey	IT
Graphic support and documentation	Facility services
Patent analysis	Communication/PR

Figure 8.1. Different Types of Support

In an innovation culture, there is a lot of focus on projects. Working on projects tends to have a higher status than working with project support. However, this is unfortunate because the support functions play an important role in the

C. Sehested, H. Sonnenberg, *Lean Innovation*, DOI 10.1007/978-3-642-15895-7_9,
© Springer-Verlag Berlin Heidelberg 2011

innovation system as a whole. If this goes unrecognized, the support functions can quickly become a place where the work is requested too late and where it is unclear what the request involves. There is a serious risk that the requests will just be added to the pile in an overfilled in-basket. Once that happens, support can easily become a bottleneck, causing delays to the projects.

There is often untapped potential in making the support functions an active player. Like the other participants in the innovation system, the support functions help create the business results that enable fast and innovative solutions.

By working with the support functions, questioning how things are done or optimizing collaboration with the projects, it is possible to find new solutions that can make the innovation process more efficient. When it comes to project support and efficiency in the innovation process, there are two main problems:

- How do you make communication between the support functions and the projects more efficient?
- How do you make the support functions' own processes more efficient?

In the following, we will take a closer look at how lean can be used to work with these two issues.

Give Projects and Support Functions a Common Objective

Support functions and projects are organized differently and have different success criteria. This, in itself, can give rise to challenges in their cooperative relationship.

Sometimes the primary objective of the support functions is to provide operational support, while project support is a secondary task. This impacts on the projects and can make the project staff feel that they are not receiving the priority and service they need. On the other hand, support functions perform tasks for more than one project, are bound by agreements with the other projects and cannot always reprioritize every time changes are made one individual project. Furthermore, the projects are often not good enough at planning and meeting deadlines, which is disruptive to the workflow of the support function and ultimately creates waste.

To get cooperation on the right track, it can be a good idea to start by giving something. A relationship that is only transactional does not bring the best out of both parties. The projects need to recognize support's role and value and they need to help them understand why their contribution is important. The project requesting the work has a responsibility. And so does the support function carrying out the request. The following figure illustrates how you can start by clarifying the roles and responsibilities for improving cooperation.

Project	Support
• Forward thinking – when is support necessary?	• Get involved – understand the customer and go to gemba
• Involve support in planning	• Insist on understanding the task and what the project is requesting
• Make sure tasks involve creative challenges	
• Maximum use of supports' competencies	• Confirm task
• Make sure support understands value and objective of the project	• Be proactive about the task's possibilities and limitations
	• Be flexible and realistic about resources
• Clearly define task – define task in dialog	• Suggest alternative solutions – challenge opinions

Figure 8.2. Improved Cooperation Between Projects and Project Support

The project manager can strengthen cooperation informally by involving the support functions in the project and making them part of the project's success. For example, the support functions can be invited to participate in the front loading workshops or the visual planning of the project. The support functions can have their own track in the visual plan that also gives them obligations and a sense of responsibility for achieving the milestones.

Often, the support staff do not really know what they are helping to create – they are just doing a job. The project team can do more to involve the support staff in the project and let them experience how their contribution is helping the customers or the company.

Another approach is to invite the support functions to work on the project physically. There is no doubt that physical distance also affects how involved the support staff feel in the project. So arranging to have a support staff member physically present in the project room at a specific time every week would promote more co-ownership.

Simplify Interaction through Standardization

Another possibility for achieving a more transparent interaction is to define the support functions' services more formally. This will clarify what the projects and the support organization have agreed on, so that specific agreements will not be necessary every time a request is sent to the support function. It may seem a bit rigid, but in practice this has proven a good way to simplify cooperation.

When standardizing tasks, it can be a good idea to specify what information the support function needs from the person requesting the work. To this end, a simple order form can sometimes be a solution.

ECCO carried out a series of workshops between projects and support functions to improve cooperation and optimize the process for initiating tasks. Staff from both the projects and the support functions were skeptical about what effect it could have and what kind of value it would give them. But their attitudes soon changed when they learned that the projects provided far too much information to the support functions and that a template could simplify the task defining process significantly.

There is often a lot of waste associated with transferring tasks, and as we have touched on earlier, eliminating unnecessary work is a simple way to improve the process. In the above example, the support functions were asked to define the kind of information they need to execute the tasks. It turned out that old conventions for good professional practice, combined with good diligent employees, created an unnecessary workload for the projects.

SLA – Service Level Agreements

In some cases, the interface between projects and support functions can be optimized by working with more formal agreements. An SLA is a cooperation agreement that defines the service deliverables. The agreement is formulated in a document and approved by both parties. An SLA makes the work more formal and ensures that the parties communicate properly what they expect from each other. An SLA can also function as a communication tool in larger organizations that need to inform large numbers of people throughout the organization about the process for a given task.

SLAs and documentation have many positive effects, but it is important to remember that they also have a tendency to create a distance between the parties. The proximity, understanding and flexibility that comes with talking about needs and possibilities can be lost if you are not careful.

A Proactive Support Function

In many instances, the support function can play a more active role in the orga-nization's performance. Because the support function supports several projects at once, they can think cross-organizationally and have a chance to improve and optimize how the company works.

A good example of the active role of the support functions comes from a pharmaceutical company. Two projects requested studies in connection with the development of their respective drugs. The support function decided to ask for more information about the studies and learn more about the content. They discovered that both studies could be carried out at the same time on the same culture medium, because the substances did not interact with each other.

Another example comes from a test department that tests equipment before it goes into production. The relevant manager received the equipment for test-ing, which repeatedly contained the same type of error. The manager analyzed the problem and discovered that there was a high staff turnover rate in the soft-ware department that developed the equipment. As a solution to the problem, he asked his staff to draw up a guide for the software staff, explaining how they could avoid such errors in future.

In both cases, the support function is an active player that takes responsibil-ity for the efficiency of the innovation process.

Overview of Processes and Capacity

There is often plenty of potential to increase efficiency and avoid conflicts by working with capacity and staff planning in the interface between projects and support functions.

The support functions become better players when they understand their internal work processes and have a good idea of the resources it takes to solve the various types of tasks. It is also helpful if they understand their own capac-ity and, perhaps, can transform that into a takt. The projects can then take the support functions' takt into account in their own planning.

There are many different ways to communicate about capacity and plan-ning. However, a good way to keep it simple is to make the capacity booking visual (Figure 8.3). A simple visual board that communicates capacity and takt can be very helpful for improving cooperation between projects and sup-port functions.

Figure 8.3. Visual Task Management on Boards

Optimizing the Support Functions

In a lean culture, the support functions, like all other processes, should work with continuous improvements. However, this can involve certain challenges. The support function staff are generally very good at operations, which, of course, is what they are recruited for. But when it comes to developing new processes and methods, they often have something to learn. The process needs to be given a little push with requirements from management as well as competence development. The manager should be the anchor for such a process, because thinking in terms of development mostly doesn't come naturally to the staff.

In many cases, it is also a good idea to ask the customers – i.e. the projects – what can be done better. Often the support functions can learn a lot from how the projects work with continuous improvements. Some of the projects' improvement ideas will deal with relations to the support functions. This is a perfect opportunity for the support functions to embrace these improvement ideas and use them to develop the service they provide to the projects. It is also a good idea to involve the projects in the development of solutions to facilitate a dialog between the parties. For example, a solution might require that both parties change how they do certain things.

The process of improving relations between projects and support does not have to be restricted to the confines of the company. To illustrate this, we would like to give an example from LINAK:

In many of their projects, LINAK had trouble with the production of tools from subsuppliers, which generally operated with delivery times of 12 to 16 weeks. This had a negative effect on LINAK's reaction time. So in a specific project, they invited some of their regular suppliers to a workshop (Note: They put competing suppliers in same room). At the workshop, LINAK hung up their work process on the wall. The suppliers did the same, and then the processes were reviewed step by step.

The ambition for the meeting was to reduce the lead time from 16 weeks to eight. The workshop revealed that by improving the processes and communication they could achieve the eight-week delivery time.

Support functions are often more operations-oriented than projects, so in this context there is a lot to be gained from looking at how lean is used in production processes.

Examples of Lean in Support Functions

In the following, we would like to give a few examples of how lean has inspired companies to make support functions more efficient.

We will look at:
- Optimizing interaction between projects and support
- Reducing lead time in the documentation process
- Doubling capacity with takt and visual management

Optimizing Interaction Between Projects and Support

At ECCO, the different development teams are organized to focus on market-related target groups. One team, the 'Ladies Team', is responsible for developing new shoe models for women. One of their projects involved developing a new shoe to replace an extraordinarily successful shoe model. However, due to pressure from the sales organization, the new model had to be developed at a much faster pace than they were used to.

The project team, which primarily comprised staff from branding, design and development, had to work efficiently with a large number of people from different support functions to succeed with this development project. Some of the support functions in play were CAD modeling, mould construction, prototype team, testing and quality. Cooperation between the project and support had previously suffered from misunderstandings, not only linguistically but also culturally, because much of the development work took place abroad. Another hurdle was differences in professional habits and department priorities. To improve the cooperation, and thereby avoid delays in the project, the project manager invited all project members and all key support staff to a workshop. The participants were asked to bring with them all the forms and information they normally used to communicate with each other.

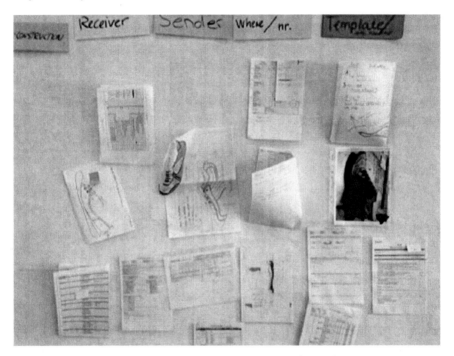

Figure 8.4. Examples of Documents Exchanged Between Project and Support

All the important interactions were mapped on the wall. The involved parties then split up into pairs to discuss how they each cooperated and find out which information in the templates was most essential. They discovered that much of the information was never used. They also found out that the same information was communicated in many different ways. And finally, they found improvement potential in how they generally cooperated and communicated with each other. They introduced two specific improvements in the relations between projects and support:

- A number of templates were simplified and approved by all parties.
- A new rule was introduced: Always call the recipient as soon as possible after sending an e-mail to explain needs and show appreciation.

The workshop and the joint discussion about improvements made it clear that the projects and support functions were playing on the same team and had the same overall objective. These specific initiatives reduced both waste and mis-understandings, and helped improve project speed.

Reducing Lead Time in the Documentation Process

At Ramboll Oil & Gas, the documentation department provides support to other departments and for the customer by updating drawings. For a long time, the department had experienced an increasing number of 'cases' in the form of drawing updates, and the tasks were seriously piling up. The was a general feeling in the department that the situation was out of control. It was a strain on the staff, and many felt that they were nothing more than "just support". One employee explained:

> *"We are always the last resort, both inhouse and for the customer, because our job is 'just' to update the drawings. We are constantly behind on our work, and when new projects come in, we sometimes have to go to a colleague from another department or the customer for missing information. And then, when our questions have been answered, we have to start all over again. It's not very inspiring."*

A large number of cases were delayed, and the customer therefore decided to introduce a registration process in an effort to 'follow the case'. Consequently, in addition to updating the drawings, the staff had to register every time a trans-action took place in the flow of a case. The registrations were sent on a weekly basis via e-mail to the customer to be used at internal departmental meetings, status meetings etc. But in the end there was no visible status. The customer required ten-day delivery, and the department was far from reaching that target.

In lean, control and registration are waste, and they are often a symptom that the process is not under control. The first step was therefore to map the process and determine the actual lead time for a case. The entire support func-tion participated in a mapping exercise. It was a real eye-opener for everyone to discover how many changes they could make themselves.

The mapping in the department resulted in a common understanding of the process flow, a number of standards for small and large tasks and the merging of certain work functions. After six months, they could see a reduction in lead time from 102 days to 17 days. This was much closer to the customer's expectations. But Rome wasn't built in a day, and the improvement process in the documentation department continued.

The two biggest changes for the department were the introduction of a daily measurement board and visual flow. Earlier management was spreadsheet-based showing all the past months, and they responded much too late to the situation. With the introduction of the measurement board, the support department became forward-looking based on daily measurements of productivity and quality. At the same time, a visual shelf system always showed exactly where a case was in the process at any given time, and whether resources needed to be redistributed in relation to case type. The previous week's results and improvement ideas are now discussed at weekly meetings, and acted on jointly.

The documentation department at Ramboll Oil & Gas created a burning platform by placing customer value at the centre, and the mapping process opened the staff's eyes to the fact that there was actually something they could do themselves. The change agent was the head of department who initiated the process and learned quite a few things along the way.

Prioritize Processes on the Critical Path

It is possible for the support functions to contribute significantly to improving the innovation work in knowledge-based organizations. A lean process often reveals a great many things that can be improved. If you need to allocate resources, it can be a good idea to make improvement ideas on the critical path your highest priority.

We have seen many examples of companies that have implemented changes to cut-back on resources or to improve the quality of the work. These are good and legitimate improvements. But starting there can have a negative effect on motivation. There is a real risk that those savings will be eaten up elsewhere in the organization, and that the quality improvements will not be visible to the outside. But if, like LINAK, you can reduce a process on the critical path from 16 weeks to eight weeks, then you have done something that clearly creates value for everyone in the company. It will also be visible to the customers and will give the company a competitive edge.

Furthermore, the positive energy it creates can be used drive subsequent improvements.

Doubling Capacity with Takt and Visual Management

As part of a lean project, ECCO took a closer look at the interaction between the projects and the department that produced the moulds for casting shoe soles. The projects were not satisfied with the time it took for the mould department to deliver the moulds. And there were large fluctuations in delivery times from project to project. The mould department felt that the criticism was unfounded because they worked hard for the projects and often experienced periods with very heavy workloads, including weekend work. Several solutions were considered, including hiring more staff in the mould department and outsourcing part of the support work to external subsuppliers.

Ultimately, ECCO decided to improve the situation and initiated an analysis of the number of moulds that were ordered by the projects in the past six months. The results of the analysis are illustrated in the following figure.

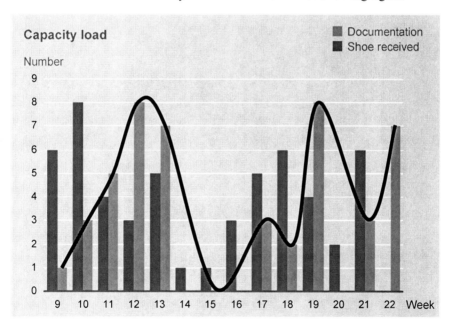

Figure 8.5. Registering How Much the Project Portfolio Draws on the Support Function

They were not too surprised to find great fluctuations in the number of orders. But what really surprised them was the fluctuations in number of moulds per order. The actual conditions had been blurred by both a very informal order routine and significant fluctuations in the department's delivery times. Thus, in a week with many orders, the orders would stack up and the delivery times would be extended, while a week with few orders resulted in shorter delivery times.

The analysis revealed that capacity in the mould department was sufficient, if the pressure on the department could be spread out more. In fact, they could nearly double the capacity. It was assessed to be important that the support department could guarantee delivery to the projects. On the other hand, the projects had to do a better job coordinating their orders for moulds.

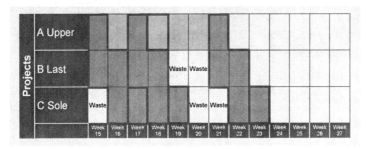

Figure 8.6. Visual Capacity Planning with Weekly Takt

Part of the solution involved determining and being explicit about the department's capacity (x moulds a week) and then making the takt visible to the projects. This allowed the projects to book specific delivery slots. An effort was also made to stagger the projects so that their needs for moulds did not overlap as much.

Literature:

Rother, M., J. Shook : Learning to See: Value Stream Mapping Add to Value and Eliminate MUDA. Spiral-Bound, 1999.
Shuker, T. & D. Tapping: *Value Stream Management for the Lean Office*. Productivity Press, 2003.

Part IV
Starting the Development Process

Chapter 9
Fast from Knowledge to Value

This book has touched upon many different aspects of lean innovation and has presented several viewpoints based on our experience from lean projects. But no two companies are alike. This is important to acknowledge when you begin the process of improving how you innovate.

Toyota, which has worked with lean for a generation, is a good source of inspiration. So are many of the international companies we refer to throughout the book. It is not about finding out what others have done and then copying it. That makes just as little sense as transferring lean from the production environment directly to innovation. The goal is to find and define the type of lean that best matches the company's visions and targets for innovation. To this end, you need to have a common understanding of which aspects are well functioning in the current processes and which should be improved to realize the strategies. Is the company doing something completely new by stepping back and analyzing its own work processes, or does the company already have a great deal of experience evaluating how they work?

Lean innovation is not a destination you can just check off once you get there. Lean innovation is a journey that never ends. It is a voyage to discover how you can, in an appreciative way, help yourself and others to improve – constantly. And even at mighty Toyota, which is considered the third most innovative company in the world after Apple and Google, the employees continue to improve how they work. Lean innovation can have a significant impact on employee and customer satisfaction, and on the company's bottom line. Especially if it is implemented in a way that is gentle and appreciative in addition to being structured and focused.

With this chapter, we provide some general advice on how to begin working with lean innovation, and then we give the floor to the leaders of the case companies, because, to a large extent, this book is based on their experience.

Understanding Strategic and Individual Motivation

A good place to start the development process is to figure out why you are even interested in initiating improvements in the innovation area. Throughout the

C. Sehested, H. Sonnenberg, *Lean Innovation*, DOI 10.1007/978-3-642-15895-7_10,
© Springer-Verlag Berlin Heidelberg 2011

journey, you will be challenged again and again, and forced to make priorities. Consequently, it is necessary to make sure everyone understands why the improvement process has been initiated. It should be possible to explain why the company needs to work with lean innovation. Do you leave on a journey because you are unhappy where you are, or because you love to travel, meet new people and see things you have never seen before?

To be successful with lean innovation, a lot of people must follow the same vision. Therefore, you need to understand what motivates and inspires various parts of the organization. It is possible that not everyone should be given a chance to speak in a lengthy democratic process. But management, or the initiators of the lean innovation process, should make an effort to understand the many different opinions and needs that can be incorporated into the vision for the lean project. To do this, you need to take a closer look at both the strategic motivation as well as the motivation among management and employees for creating better innovation processes.

The Strategic Motivation

Before introducing lean innovation in a company, it is critical that you find out how essential this particular area is in relation to other strategic objectives, such as streamlining production, branding or upgrading the SAP or CRM systems. You need to assess which elements of the business strategy are to be supported by lean innovation and why. This requires an insightful strategy process and an excellent understanding of market developments and the actual potential of the organization. A solid strategy is a good point of departure for setting a relevant ambition for the innovation area and the lean process. You need to know what the most important ambition is. Possible innovation ambitions:

- To improve the customer experience by delivering the solutions in a new way
- To react quickly and more powerful in a changed market
- To increase output and the innovation rate of new solutions
- To be better at solving tasks cross-site in a global organization
- To improve the quality of the individual solutions

The Motivation of Management

Management represents the owners and the strategic needs. But lean innovation will also give rise to changes in the behavior of even the management team. Here, we are thinking about the top management, which is often a key factor in the change process. It is therefore important to understand what motivates them.

There may be a need for a joint project to bring the management team closer together. They may want to increase the dynamics in the innovation area by working with continuous improvements. Or they may be looking for a way to get the employees to assume more responsibility for the development of the company.

The individual manager may also be motivated by a desire to develop his or her leadership skills in interaction with colleagues by trying out things in new situations. Lean will give many managers the opportunity to step out of their discipline-oriented comfort zone and do even more to help their employees boost their skills.

The Motivation of Employees

In our experience, it is often the employees who like lean the most, once they understand what it is. This is because lean emphasizes the importance of their work. Lean focuses on what they do, i.e. on the daily value creation. Lean recognizes their insights and gives them the tools, training and processes to increase their value creation. Lean innovation creates processes and structures for the necessary standard tasks, so there is more room for creative value generation. Intelligent lean innovation can reduce stress and increase employee satisfaction. But what do the employees say? In the process of defining the lean initiative, it is important to hear their input and to integrate their wishes and needs into the foundation and objectives of the development project.

Defining Clear Objectives

The shared ambitions of executive management that have triggered the company's interest in lean innovation should be discussed, clarified and considered from all angles in the relevant fora. Some companies may also benefit from involving their customers in this process. Once a common understanding has been established in the leadership team, it is a good idea to formulate official project objectives. Just like for any other knowledge project, the following should be defined:

- Purpose – Why are we doing it?
- Success criteria – How do we determine whether it is a success?
- Project deliverables – What should be the specific output of the project?

Precise objectives are important, especially when communicating to a wider audience. It is also a good idea if you find yourself during the journey having trouble remembering why you embarked on it in the first place. The initiators of the process should return to the objective on a regular basis to make sure the ambition level can be upheld and to make any necessary adjustments.

The objectives of the lean innovation initiative should harmonize with how you initiate the work. Linear thinkers might be of the opinion that the objective always comes first before the plan. But in practice, change is an iterative process, and you need to work with both the objectives and the process at the same time.

Choosing the Right Approach

When defining the lean initiative, you should think very carefully about the possible approaches. In the following, we will look at a model for the overall implementation strategy. Then, we will highlight a few challenges which may be valuable to consider in the beginning, but also throughout the lean project.

Choosing an Implementation Strategy

You are playing with powerful forces when you start to change something as fundamental as knowledge work. Within the organization, there are so many different stakeholders and opinions about the subject that you easily lose control over the process. You risk doing too little in some areas or simply addressing the wrong issues. Not only should the lean project have room for comprehensive learning and commitment, it is also necessary to have a clear objective and implementation strategy. Figure 9.1 presents some of the things you need to think about before getting started. The model shows four alternative approaches to the implementation project: 'big bang', 'domino', 'cascade' and 'small steps'.

Deciding which approach is best depends on the purpose, ambition level, organizational structure, competencies and experiences from previous change projects. The different strategies can be combined, for example part of the project can be implemented as 'small steps', while another part is implemented as 'big bang'.

An example of 'small steps' is choosing a specific innovation project (part of the organization) and applying lean thinking by introducing only some of the lean methods (part of the solution). The objective of 'small steps' may be to learn more about lean innovation and to create ambassadors within the organization.

This can be a good way to get the process going quickly, and if you choose the right processes, you will quickly produce successes that can pave the way for other initiatives. The drawback is that you start with small steps at the lowest level in the organization, which does not give managers much experience with lean innovation. With 'small steps', management does not play an active role in defining the working method and culture that should characterize the innovation processes. In this situation, lean innovation can end up being nothing more than a tool project that does not help the organization understand the essence.

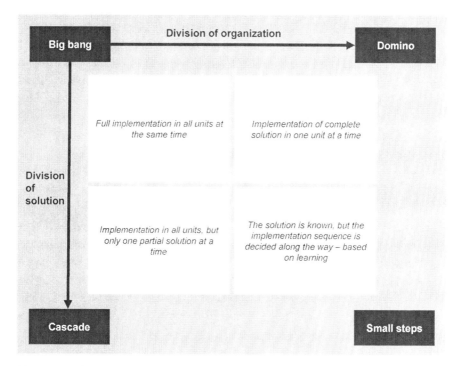

Figure 9.1. Alternative Implementation Strategies

Sometimes the 'big bang' method is the right strategy to begin with. Because it signals great importance, it is sometimes easier with this approach to force a general dialog among the managers about the future culture and working methods. For example, every manager can be assigned tasks which they work with personally and in their department. Then, they can give each other feedback on this process and share their experiences across the organization. In this way, innovation projects and support functions become part of the lean project, and everyone gets more responsible for contributing to the strategic changes in the innovation process.

The 'big bang' approach seems to indicate that a lasting cultural change is possible through a short and intensive project. But this is not realistic. On the other hand, the 'big bang' approach can be a good way to shake the organization free or get people from all over the organization involved after testing certain solutions on a smaller scale. But before you begin, you should make sure you have the staffing and resources to support a broad implementation on all fronts at the same time.

The 'cascade' model is a variation on the 'big bang' that divides the objective up into smaller pieces. For example, the changes might be incorporated into a campaign structure where implementation across the organization takes place in waves – a subset of development steps that the entire organization undergoes. This is cross-organizational involvement in minor steps. Individual solution elements can be brought into play successively. For example, you can focus on implementing visual planning in all projects, and then introducing front loading, continuous improvements, objective-driven behavior etc. With the 'cascade' model, a takt for implementation is established. And with every beat, the whole organization is touched.

In the 'domino' model, one unit is completed at a time. For example, you could implement all changes in one department or one geographical location at a time. This might be the right approach if there is not unanimous support to proceed, or if you do not have the resources to work across the entire organization at the same time. However, one drawback is that you can inadvertently create a '*not invented here*' atmosphere in those areas of the company that were not involved from the beginning. This can cost you time later, because they may not feel like having an influence on the implementation and, thus, resist the change. At the very least, you need to be prepared to start over in the new areas. You cannot expect to be able to just roll back 20 per cent and then start from there. If you choose the 'domino' model, it may be worthwhile to consider whether you can create an 'overlapping' domino effect in which the subsequent areas can become involved on a small scale to obtain insight along the way, so that they do not have to start entirely from scratch.

Involve the Customers from the Beginning

We have seen many improvement projects start out with customer value as part of their objectives only to shift to an increasingly internal focus. This kind of development is unfortunate in a lean innovation project. Because, naturally, when aiming to more efficiently develop products and services, customer focus is a central aspect.

A good way to ensure customer focus is by involving your customers in lean innovation from the beginning and allowing them to participate in the dialog about how you can improve. One thing that can keep companies from doing this are the perceived risks and consequences of approaching the customer and explaining to them that you are in the process of improving how you work. No one wants to put their weaknesses on display. Furthermore, the customer may subsequently expect to see noticeable changes and may contact you after a few months to ask how the process is going.

Another concern is that you may not be able to stick to the lean innovation process and will later be forced to explain to the customer that their input might not be used after all. But despite the potential difficulties that come with involving the customers, we still recommend it. The changes will have a greater impact if everyone understands the customer's priorities. At the same time, it allows you to train a key lean muscle at the implementation stage by "going to gemba" to learn from real life where your products meet the customers.

Create Results that Customers Can See

This consideration is aiming at creating customer value fast. You should begin the process in the area that is most visible to customers and where you can achieve the fastest impact.

In practice, this means starting with the most important projects. However, we see a lot of companies choose to start with processes which lie outside the scope of the projects and which will only increase customer value in the long term. Taking a long perspective and viewing lean as a long-term investment is fine, however this approach can also cause you to start working on something that is actually not particularly important. We recommend concentrating on whatever creates fast successes and results in fast customer response.

Focus on Reducing Development Time

"Vodka is luxury we have. Caviar is a luxury we have. Time is not." This was Khrushchev's response to a request to discuss strategy with a political officer in the middle of a decisive battle in 1941 in the fight for Leningrad during World War II. The effect of lean on projects can be measured by three criteria: time, deliverables (quality) and resources (costs). Unless specific challenges indicate otherwise, you − like Khrushchev − should always focus on time first. Reducing lead time helps reveal any waste in the organization. Many projects become both more expensive and deliver lower quality because they are allowed to run on for too long.

One strategy is to take the company's most important project and define a target for completing it in half the time. From there, it is a matter of determining which sub-projects, sub-processes or support processes need to be optimized to achieve this target. This helps ensure that the improvements initiated have a visible effect and improve the company's competitiveness and ability to react.

Make Management a Driver and Role Model

If you have ambitions to adopt lean, either fully or partially, as your corporate and management culture, the management team may as well start practicing right away.

They do not have to be experts in lean from the outset. It is okay for management to announce their intentions to begin improving how they work. Subsequently, they will be implementing some initiatives that should ultimately create a culture with continuous improvement as a core principle. Management is in the midst of a learning process and, along with the rest of the company, they have initiated a process that everyone should get better at over time. It ought to be possible to send out this kind of message in a development-oriented, knowledge-based company.

Some knowledge-based companies only view lean as a tool to be implemented lower in the organization close to the value-creating processes. The consequence of this attitude, however, is that management does not get sufficiently involved in the lean implementation process. Instead, managers leave, perhaps, 90 per cent of the implementation process up to lean agents – employees trained in lean concepts and methods. They may even give the project manager job to the youngest employee, who is not sufficiently appreciated for his or her professional competencies.

Unfortunately, this means that management is not leading the way. In this way, management is sending, perhaps unknowingly, a signal that improving innovation is not important. And by not getting involved, managers are not learning anything about what lean actually is. The managers have no personal knowledge of how difficult it is to change and, especially, to maintain change. Thus, they have problems motivating the knowledge workers who are fighting to implement the lean ideals.

In addition, inexperienced lean agents are often not respected enough. The agents are tasked with developing the work processes of other successful employees, and that is difficult because people – especially highly intelligent people – are skeptical and can feel intimidated by being told what to do by a less-respected employee. If you choose to use lean agents, it is vital that they are both professional and leadership role models within the organization.

Let the Case Companies Inspire You

Thousands of companies throughout the world already have experience with lean innovation. Together, all the employees involved in lean innovation in these companies represent a vast experience base.

Companies interested in working with lean innovation need to come to their own realizations and acquire their own learning. But the experiences of other companies can be a good source of inspiration when deciding how to proceed. In the following, we would like to present the most essential lessons that ECCO, LINAK, Ramboll Oil & Gas, Exhausto and Coloplast have learned from this process.

We want to emphasize that all five companies have achieved good results with lean. And we would like to thank them for sharing their experiences, both good and bad, with the readers of this book.

Comments from Aage Andersen, ECCO

"I'm pleased that we have established cross-organizational cooperation. We have created a set-up that involves the employees across the organization and have established cross-functional teams. Generally, I'd say it was good that we worked with a pilot area and focused on quickly creating success stories.

Looking at what we could have done differently, there is not doubt that it's important to get the management team involved and to make them understand what the process is all about and what role they must play in a lean organization. They need to know what lean innovation is. It's absolutely crucial that they support the process from the very beginning. We should also have been better at defining solid objectives from the outset. That would have made it easier to see where we should focus our energy. For example, in the pilot area, we knew we wanted to improve our lead time – so we knew where we had to go.

My three pieces of advice for anyone starting up a lean innovation process is to get the support of the management team and make sure they understand what it involves. Management needs to get into the game. Define a clear objective. Finally, it's a good idea to concentrate on one specific area rather than try to do it all at once. This can be done in many ways. Just don't bite off more than you can chew and try to save the whole world at once."

Comments from Claus Sørensen, LINAK

"We did a good job getting a team up and running quickly. We also decided to make lean innovation a whole-hearted effort and allocate the necessary resources to the project. Another thing we did pretty well was to take a flexible approach to lean innovation. We modified the implementation process several times. For example, after a period with pilot projects, we decided to launch the initiative throughout the entire organization. We realized this was necessary because the same people working on different projects were confused by having to do things one way on one project and another way on another project.

Looking back, we probably should have defined the objectives more clearly. More importantly, we should have ensured stronger agreement within top management, and we should have been better at breaking the targets down into sub-targets. This would have allowed us to run shorter and more concentrated sub-projects in our lean program. I think that would have produced even better success stories within the organization.

My advice to others who are just getting started is to devote energy to clarifying why they want to implement lean. If they have already started the process and feel a need to revitalize it, I would ask them, "Why?". My second piece of advice is that you need to have people who are committed to the process and who have the right competencies. If you can't find both qualities in the same people, then I'd say a strong sense of commitment is the most important."

Comments from Anders Rødgaard Knudsen, Ramboll Oil & Gas

"We were good at getting the management team involved as genuine driving forces. We ran a total of eight workshop days to help them understand lean innovation in our context. That was a wise move, because now we can see that the ownership is solid and stretches down to middle management and project management. It was good that we provided time for management to express doubts and ask questions before involving the rest of the organization. Furthermore, we chose to audit the project managers in their ability to implement lean innovation, which increased the speed of the roll-out.

Lean innovation has gone very well, but if we had to do it again, I think we should have changed two things. Firstly, we shouldn't have implemented it sequentially, the way we did. We started by implementing lean completely in one location, and then moved on to the next. This produced and understandable a sense of "not invented here" in some areas, which we could have lived without. Secondly, it was a challenge that I, as a lean program owner, was not sufficiently involved in the process and the management fora in all locations.

My advice to others is to introduce lean to the management team before the employees. Management needs to understand that lean is not a toolbox, but a leadership philosophy about continuous improvements supported by tools. Management will most likely not be able to continue working as they used to, and that is something they need to accept."

Comments from Karsten Lund, Exhausto

"We started out slowly with articles, books and conferences to find out more about what lean means for R&D work. This gave us a good foundation for the subsequent process. And when we finally got started, we spent a good deal of time discussing what the most important goals were for our innovation. And that worked really well. We defined seven goals, including product quality, time-to-market, business case and risk management. We discussed the fact that some of the goals pull in opposite directions and established a balanced set of innovation KPIs.

We started out like a grassroots movement in the development department. We should have done a better job involving the rest of the organization in order to establish a greater sense of ownership more quickly. We underestimated the need for the participation of such departments as manufacturing and marketing.

My first piece of advice to people interested in lean is to find or create people who are dedicated to the process. Successfully implementing lean innovation requires an extraordinary effort. It is not just a couple of hours here and there. I would also recommend establishing understanding and ownership early, from areas such as manufacturing, marketing, sales and service. This can be done by jointly mapping the entire innovation process and getting a shared understanding of where the strengths and waste lie."

Comments from John Raabo Nielsen, Coloplast

One good thing we did was to quickly realize that our lack of experience with lean innovation and the lack of external benchmarks made it necessary to continuously adjust our method. It was also positive that we appointed a highly experienced American consultant as head of our lean innovation function. This created a very efficient knowledge transfer process with limited investment.

With what we know today, we should probably have stared out more pragmatically with less focus on structures and preliminary studies. We should also have placed more emphasis on more application-oriented staff training, for example by taking on the actual projects sooner. We focused for too long on process mapping before deciding where we wanted to make changes. We should also have come up with a simpler and more practical way to involve the managers.

My advice to others who are just getting started is to keep it simple! I also think that the line management should assume responsibility for the change process. And it is important to get as many employees as possible to use lean – especially in the management team. Make lean innovation something that can be applied in practice with apprenticeship training of employees instead of 'classroom' training. I recommend taking a positive approach to the process instead of starting out by focusing on the negative."

Literature:

Kotter, John P.: *Leading Change*. Harvard Business School Publishing, 1996.

Postscript
Fueled by a Dream

In 1990, Womack and Jones formulated the first structured arguments in favor of lean production in their book *The Machine that Changed the World* . Their next book *Lean Thinking* came six years later and really spread the word about lean. Today, you won't find many production companies that have not implemented lean production. However, lean innovation is a more recent development and has not yet caught on in the same way as lean production. But we see more and more examples of companies that have successfully implemented lean in their knowledge work.

The potential for developing knowledge-based organizations and processes is enormous – both because it takes place early in the value chain and because more and more people will work with knowledge and fewer with production. So the question is not whether there will be a big breakthrough but when and how it will come.

In 1990, Womack and Jones claimed that it took more than 50 years to spread the idea of mass production, and they asked how long it would take lean production to reach every corner of the world. They assumed it would happen within ten years. In fact, it took nearly 20 years, but the impact on global competition has been overwhelming.

So how long will it take for lean innovation to spread? It is difficult to say. But one thing is certain, the need for innovation is greater today than ever before. Pressure from global competition and developing countries will increase. It is simply crucial, especially for the old economies, that we learn to innovate more efficiently. Anyone who has worked in Asia knows the aspiration and energy that we are up against. There is no doubt that these countries are open to introducing new ways of working that can boost the effect of the employees' specialist knowledge. We therefore encourage all companies to take the competition seriously and get started on an ambitious improvement process, also within knowledge work.

There are stars out there in the form of companies that have achieved fantastic results because they have been able to create a culture that brings unique solutions to the market. We all know who they are, but there are many more

C. Sehested, H. Sonnenberg, *Lean Innovation*, DOI 10.1007/978-3-642-15895-7,
© Springer-Verlag Berlin Heidelberg 2011

companies that work "down to earth" and make progress one day at a time. These companies or their employees might feel like they do not have a chance to become stars. But they do. And the way forward is to have an ambition to make innovation something different and more than it is today. Without that ambition, it does not make much sense to initiate a learning process in which they get better and better day by day. But with that ambition, lean innovation can be the path that brings the company closer to the stars. There is everything to be gained, on both a financial and human level. Your customers will be more satisfied, your work will be more gratifying and your relationship with your colleagues will be better.

Some people resist lean innovation because the perceive an unsolvable dilemma between innovation and lean and between creativity and efficiency. The purpose of this book is to demonstrate that there is no dilemma. It is our hope that the readers can use this book to overcome their own skepticism and that of others and that they can launch a development which increases both the speed and predictability of their innovation processes.

We hope the reader will be motivated to embark on this journey with their colleagues, just like people did in the 15th century from the Port of Cádiz, fueled by a common dream. The only difference is that today we encourage the travelers to divide their journey up into smaller stages and bring home the bounty as they go along rather than wait to cash in until the very end.

"The greatest danger for most of us is not that our aim is too high and we miss it, but that it is too low, and we reach it."
Michelangelo

CLAUS SEHESTED is partner with Implement Consulting Group. He has managed a number of lean innovation programs in larger industry and service corporations. Claus started his career in Danfoss A/S and Tektronix Inc. He holds a PhD from Technical University of Denmark and Technische Universität München. He has worked with strategy, organizational and business development across Europe, United States and Asia. Claus is author on several publications about innovation and product development.

HENRIK SONNENBERG is working as management consultant with Implement Consulting Group, focusing on strategy and innovation processes. Across Europe and Asia he managed initiatives within product strategy, product development and manufacturing effectiveness. He is educated machinist, mechanical engineer, and hold an MBA from Carlson School at University of Minnesota. Henrik is author of the crime novel "Ghettoen", ex-graffiti artist and currently a capable off-piste snowboarder.

Breinigsville, PA USA
17 November 2010

249491BV00010B/31/P

9 783642 158940